Key to Part Two Pric

Under £150

A £0–50
B £50–100
C £100–150

£150–750

D £150–250
E £250–350
F £350–450
G £450–600
H £600–750

Over £750

J £750–1,000
K £1,000–2,000
L £2,000–5,000
M Over £5,000

Unless otherwise stated, the coded prices given in this book are for pieces of furniture in good condition. Prices fluctuate, with damaged items frequently going for less money or first rate examples in excellent condition fetching twice the suggested amount. On the whole, estimates given reflect prices reached in the saleroom; if buying from a dealer it will be necessary to take his profit into consideration.

ANTIQUE FURNITURE ON A BUDGET

GRAHAM SHEARING

ANTIQUE FURNITURE ON A BUDGET

A Practical Guide to Furnishing Your Home

EBURY PRESS
LONDON

TO MY PARENTS

First published 1980 by Ebury Press
National Magazine House,
72 Broadwick Street,
London W1V 2BP

ISBN 0 85223 149 0

Drawings by Peter Fitzjohn
Designed by Derek Morrison
Edited by Patricia Mackinnon

The publishers wish to thank the following for the loan of items photographed on the jacket:

Afia Carpets Ltd for flooring; Derwent Upholstery Ltd for sofa; Hallidays Ltd for mantlepiece and other fireplace equipment; London Lighting Co Ltd for lamp; Ning Antiques for bookcase and armchair; Sugar Cane Ltd for coffee table; Murray Thomson Antiques for barometer.

Filmset by
Advanced Filmsetters (Glasgow) Ltd
Printed and bound by
Cambridge University Press

Contents

Key to Part Two Price Grades

Under £150

A £0–50
B £50–100
C £100–150

£150–750

D £150–250
E £250–350
F £350–450
G £450–600
H £600–750

Over £750

J £750–1,000
K £1,000–2,000
L £2,000–5,000
M Over £5,000

Unless otherwise stated, the coded prices given in this book are for pieces of furniture in good condition. Prices fluctuate, with damaged items frequently going for less money or first rate examples in excellent condition fetching twice the suggested amount. On the whole, estimates given reflect prices reached in the saleroom; if buying from a dealer it will be necessary to take his profit into consideration.

Introduction

THIS book did not originate in an antique shop: it started in the furniture department of a large and 'fashionable' London department store. The only difference between myself and the other people looking at the display was that while I knew a great deal more about antique furniture than modern, the casual visitors to this furniture shop were less likely to be familiar with the field of antiques. My impression was that the ordinary buyer of furniture, if looking for value for money, might be better advised at least to consider the respective merits of antique and modern pieces. He is looking for sturdy, comfortable and stylish furniture at a competitive price and seldom does he get any of these things.

A few weeks later I was in another well known London department store which caters for a less well-heeled clientèle. After studying the furniture I came to the same conclusion I had arrived at in the grander establishment. Later still, I examined the furniture in a national chain of stores at the cheaper end of the market. Having seen all of these firms and having made subsequent studies of the modern furniture market, I concluded that the interests of value for money, economy, comfort, and (less easy to define) stylishness are better served by the purchaser being offered an alternative.

I believe that antique furniture, in the widest sense, offers that alternative. The aim of this book is to put forward its competitive merits and to give a guide on the basis of which a buyer may confidently enter any antique shop.

Take a motor car, for example; the average buyer does not walk into a showroom and choose the first car that comes to hand. He will go to a bookshop or newsagent and buy a publication which acts as arbiter between one car and another. Exactly the same should happen when furniture is bought. This book compares prices and also explains the usual pitfalls, always with a view to the relative merits. With this last point in mind I must admit to having on occasion taken a preference for some modern specimens, but these occasions are rare. It is worth taking some trouble, because after buying a house and a motor car, the highest price paid by a householder is likely to be for a piece of furniture – notably a dining table or a set of dining chairs, or (usually one of the most expensive items) a lounge suite.

CATEGORIES

One of the characteristics of this book – and in particular of Part II, the major section – is its assumption that buyers of furniture can be broken down into three groups on the basis of the amount of money they are prepared to spend. Whichever group you belong to you should be able to afford an antique example of everything essential for the average house.

The first category assumes that you wish to spend less than £150 per item at today's prices (October 1980). I am talking in the main about major items such as a dining table rather than, say, a small stool. An impossible task, you might say, but even in today's inflationary spiral shrewd and thrifty buying puts such items within your grasp. It means the collector, or furniture buyer, becomes something of a hunter – often hunting against time – but this is frequently, in any case, of the essence of collecting. Since the durability of antique furniture is so much greater than that of modern (under normal use it should last longer than a lifetime) the few extra weeks or even months taken in the buying will be well spent. I have known many young couples, setting up home in a small house or flat, who are prepared to endure the inconvenience of a few months without a table rather than buying a new example precipitately, which they would soon tire of. From the financial point of view they could probably sell the table only at a considerable loss, whereas apart from the momentary loss which is the seller's profit, it is unlikely that any piece of furniture illustrated in this book will lose its value.

The second category is for buyers who are prepared to spend a little more, say between £150 and £750, on their main items of furniture. They include families with little spare money or the young professional couple – in fact many of the people who have occasion to buy furniture. Most antique dealers, recognising this as much as the department stores, cater to the heavy demand.

The third category covers furniture priced at £750 and over. Although you might think that buyers in this category would be limited, in fact it involves a wide group of people; they include those who sense that in times of inflation money is often wisely replaced by objects of an inflation-proof kind and who have started to buy and collect antique furniture, however indiscriminately. From this broad upper category a small number of examples has been selected.

Thus in Part II, under 'Dining tables' (page 57), you will find a selection of tables under £150, a similar number which fit into the £150–£750 category, and a smaller group of tables representative of the top range, £750 and over. Each table is illustrated, with a caption giving a short description and, occasionally, special points of interest or 'watchpoints'. Prices will vary from shop to shop and saleroom to saleroom so I have selected an average figure. This price has been expressed as a graded code letter rather than as a specific amount, to make further allowance for variations between dealers and for the condition of the furniture and inflation. The table of price grades (from A to M) is on page 6.

THE INVESTMENT FACTOR

Most people look on the purchase of antique furniture as an investment. Much has already been written on the relevant advantages and disadvantages, and the subject is considered at a later stage in this book. But two points are most commonly overlooked. People seldom do sell furniture originally acquired with a view to investment; the same is true of silver, glass, ceramics, and so on. A table no longer required is more usually moved to a less conspicuous position than cashed in – traditionally such pieces were moved a floor up until they reached the attic. It is unusual for such a piece to be sold, and the odd thing is that the example which replaces it will also be bought for 'investment' and be just as unlikely to be sold with a view to making a profit. The second point is that people grow attached to their furniture, even to the extent of growing blind to any defects. Look at the contents of the homes of acquaintances over the age of fifty-five – people frequently with enough money to replace the less convenient pieces of furniture. Much remains that should have been thrown away.

SKILLED INFORMATION

When you have read and absorbed the history of furniture, as outlined in Part III of this book, you may be better equipped to distinguish the finer points of style and period. But this is only partially helpful when you enter an antique shop to buy furniture. Two chapters in Part I give relevant information, Chapter 3 dealing with how to look at furniture and spot fakes, and Chapter 4 giving advice of a practical nature on the problems of restoration and conservation.

Picture two chairs: to the inexperienced eye they have no distinguishing features at all when compared with each other, but one was made in 1765 and the other in 1905. The purchaser will be anxious to ensure that he is not deluded into buying a spurious piece as a genuine one. Chapter 3 discusses circumstances when a fake or a heavily restored piece is actually worth buying and the extent to which restoration increases or decreases the value of furniture. Reproductions, as opposed to fakes and restored work, are dispassionately considered. The chapter ends with a discussion of parts of pieces of furniture (such as chair legs or stretchers) which ought to be closely examined before purchase, telling you what to look out for. The subsequent chapter is particularly useful when the purchase of an unrestored piece is contemplated (for example at an auction sale). It examines the cost of restoration, the extent to which such work can be carried out by a novice, the question of finding a restorer and, later, problems of conservation.

This information, which is not always accessible in any one book, should equip you to talk to any dealer with confidence. You will find that a dealer confronted with a prospective purchaser who is fairly knowledgeable will be that much more prepared to discuss the merits and demerits of any piece of furniture he has in stock.

FUNCTION

It is always said by the manufacturers that modern pieces of furniture fulfil the requirements of modern living more satisfactorily than any antique. The fitted kitchen and bedroom come to mind immediately, and in circumstances like these the requirements of utility and convenience are combined. However, modern is not always best. Although a kitchen made up from antique pieces may not be as functional as a modern design, it may be superior in other respects – the up-to-date is not necessarily wholly successful. Again, take the easy chair. Much research has gone into reconciling function and comfort, but a Windsor chair or a Queen Anne wing chair have already satisfied the requirements by the gradual processes of evolution.

Another relevant aspect is that, as the needs of people change, the functions of existing pieces of furniture change also. Antique furniture seems more suitable for adaptation than modern: a breakfast table from a Georgian mansion may easily serve as a dining table in a town house of today, seating twice the number for which it was originally intended; a Victorian marble-topped washstand makes an ideal sideboard in today's dining room; a mahogany Georgian corner washstand becomes a corner table, displaying flowers or bric-à-brac. And this change of function can take place with no structural alteration to the original piece.

Many of the examples of furniture included in this book are shown because their original function is redundant, the value thus diminished, and they can economically be applied to other uses. Much bedroom furniture, for example, is inexpensive today and has been used to advantage in more public rooms. In the thirties, a type of occasional table was manufactured specifically for the purpose of holding large, heavy wireless receivers. They are tall, rectangular tables with barley twist legs. Today they can be acquired for as little as five pounds and can be used for a multitude of purposes.

A LINK WITH THE PAST

Furniture evokes the past as well as if not better than pictures, artefacts of silver, glass or ceramics, or even books. Memories of grandparents are often stirred by the striking of the grandfather clock on the wall, or evoked by the polished mahogany of a familiar table. Students of literature and art will remark on how a specific period is evoked by reference to some piece of furniture. There is no reason why an interesting or even authentic period flavour cannot be created by anybody, even of limited means, provided he or she is prepared to take just a little time to prepare the ground. Pictures and small evocative objects can be gathered together for modest outlay – often as little as ten or twenty pounds – once the eye has been trained and the art of patience acquired.

Do not think that because you live in a modern house you are precluded from having any contact with the past. Countless thousands of collectors have found that such inhibitions are without foundation. Antiques can dominate the modern or they can accentuate it, and a cursory perusal of today's glossy fashion magazines only goes to emphasise the point. Men and women who have reluctantly inherited an antique or two, never having thought for a moment about such things, suddenly become totally preoccupied with the idea of collecting.

Do not think either that a growing family rules out the possession of antiques. Antique furniture is often better constructed than its modern equivalents and quite able to withstand the slings and arrows of outrageous children. The only things children are sometimes hard on are textiles and tops of tables (with ball-point pens!).

My aim is to provide some ideas which will give the reader a backdrop to a style of life he or she may like to lead. Furniture from the past does not spell formality, or mean an absence of comfort, or require a disregard for the practical, and, most important of all, it need not involve a great outlay. Predictions for the 1980s have indicated that in the field of interior decoration the prevailing styles will look to comfort, and a comforting atmosphere, as a means of enduring the forthcoming decade. I have singled out antique furniture as being one of the ways in which the style of the 1980s may be typified.

PART ONE

I

How Much Do You Want to Spend?

IN the field of antiques an old maxim, much used in autograph albums of the early years of this century, is apposite: 'Pay as you go, and if you can't pay, don't go.' For there is no facility on the lines of hire purchase available to the buyers of antique furniture and the principle of cash-on-the-nail is one that is basically undiminished.

The first question you must ask yourself is, 'How much do I want to spend?' Unfortunately the need for furniture tends to come in one fell swoop, on engagement to marry, on renting an unfurnished apartment or when buying a house or flat. Usually the householder will have very little cash indeed. You may be tempted to buy from your local furniture supermarket with its advantages of convenience and economy; this will certainly make shopping as easy as possible. When buying antique furniture you must be prepared for a good deal of trudging round shops, junk yards and salerooms, in most cases to no apparent effect.

In the area of economy it is not quite so certain that your local furniture supermarket has the edge on buying antique furniture. This comparison of prices between some modern furniture and equivalent antique pieces proves the point.

MODERN		PERIOD ANTIQUE	
Reproduction Georgian chair	£70	Morris & Co. dining chair	£35
Reproduction dining table	£200	Late Georgian solid oak dining table	£145
Chesterfield sofa	£450	Late Victorian sofa	£80
Fashionable Scandinavian-style sofa	£1,500	Late Georgian giltwood sofa	£1,100
Swedish beech dining chair	£250	Regency sabre leg dining chair	£75

In time you may have more money at your disposal and wish to buy more antique furniture. In these circumstances you may be prepared to put quite a bit of money into furniture on the assumption that while it is pleasant to look at, it also has the advantage of increasing in value, leaving the modern furniture suite standing. Finally, your income may increase so that you are able to become a major collector of the very best in furniture, or alternatively you may decide to splash out on one particular object of your fancy – perhaps with the aid of a windfall from a great aunt, or as the result of a lucky win on the horses.

Certainly a discernible series of groups of antique hunters emerges, relating both to buyers from shops or from the salerooms. As has been said in the Introduction, this grouping has been fitted into the following three price bandings: £0–£150, £150–£750 and over £750. In Part II these divisions are graphically set out at the beginning of each chapter. I have added a keyed figure to the caption to every object illustrated and this should be referred to the table on page 6 which will give a more precise indication of price within the groupings. This code form gives a more adequate indication of value: it would be foolish to give a piece of furniture an exact price when inflation is rife. The early months of 1980 have been marked by a sharp interest in antique furniture in the major London salerooms, and some high prices have been reported. However, it is thought that the major prices can be explained away by reference to some other factors unimportant to the general trend.

PRINCIPAL MOVEMENTS IN THE LOWER PRICE BANDS

Sets of chairs are no longer certain to remain within the lowest band. Cheap sets of country chairs in provincial salerooms were often sold for as little as £50 but are no longer available at such low prices. A set of six Oxford chairs, a variant on the Wycombe chair and particularly common in the region of Oxfordshire (although much more widely dispersed), is likely to be priced on the border of the next price grouping. The late Victorian lath-back Windsor chair (see page 54) remains within the range, as does a set of six Thonet bentwood chairs of the early twentieth century (see page 53).

Dining tables, the other most expensive item, are still to be found, with two well known varieties comfortably inside the lower band. First there is the pine kitchen table, of late Victorian date (see page 59), which should still cost below £100; secondly, the late Georgian dropleaf table of simple form (see page 60) which still represents outstanding value. Sofas are the other main growth area in this band and Victorian examples are now fetching high prices, especially when they are of the drop-arm variety. So while it is likely that some change will take place within this price band, at present a general state of equilibrium is to be expected.

PRINCIPAL MOVEMENTS IN THE MIDDLE PRICE BAND

The main reason why prices are rising in the middle price band is that there is a general and steady demand, not a particular desire to invest in furniture. It is a characteristic of this type of buying that although the buyers hope their purchase will be a hedge against inflation, they never have any strong desire to reap their profits on a resale. The only reason why this type of buying and selling for profit would go on in the middle band is that when a buyer resells for less than £1,000, he avoids having to pay capital gains tax on his profit. This type of business, in any case, does not really happen in furniture but rather with something like gold coins which are so much more convenient a medium for this kind of profit taking.

The articles which have recently increased extensively in price have now stabilised.

They include the Davenport, the Regency breakfast table and the Canterbury (see pages 80, 62 and 134), all well suited for the small flat. Dressers have largely moved out of the category altogether and are now safely ensconced in the upper price bracket.

PRINCIPAL MOVEMENTS IN THE UPPER PRICE BAND

The last two years have seen an extraordinary rise in the price of very fine and rare antiques and it seems most unlikely that this will stop now. Recently we have seen prices of over £100,000 being asked for good examples of English furniture in both the salerooms and in dealers' galleries. Further down the scale, high prices are noted generally, and the first two months of 1980 saw high prices paid in London salerooms for furniture which although good was not outstanding. So it appears that the upper price range is buoyant.

Dining tables and large sets of chairs have increased in value considerably; not only private buyers but also corporate bodies seek such furniture. But good antiques remain very competitive in the area of £750–£1,000. The dresser has now stabilised its price after an extraordinary spiral which lasted a good two years. French provincial furniture has a ready market in England now that fine examples of good oak have become all but unobtainable.

The latest recruits to the upper price band are somewhat remarkable, being the Elizabethan and Jacobean joint stool and a really fine mid-eighteenth century Windsor chair made of yew. Good quality specimens of each are likely to fetch over £750.

2
Where to Buy

HAVING decided how much money you have to spend the question arises as to where you should spend it? It is not a foolish question because there are a number of alternatives and there are circumstances where one is to be preferred to another. It may be that one person has a particular aptitude for buying at an auction, for it is generally agreed that this method is not for everybody. Another buyer may have a way of negotiating with a certain type of antique dealer that makes it very much to his advantage to buy in this particular way. Mainly it is from the antique dealer and in the saleroom that the buying will be done, but there is also the antique market or fair where a good deal of business can be carried out, or the more rare circumstance of the private contract between individuals. This chapter examines each of these circumstances.

THE DEALER

The person interested in buying furniture will in by far the greatest number of cases buy from an antique dealer and this is certainly to be recommended for the beginner. If he has a considerable sum of money to spend he is clearly best advised to go to a dealer of some reputation. Of course there are several kinds of dealer. The bottom grade is the local junk merchant, who is as likely to sell old electric fires and broken television sets as any antique. But within two miles of central London there are many such dealers, and one is well known for the mid-nineteenth-century elm-seated chairs which he regularly sells for five pounds. The same is true of most towns and villages throughout the British Isles, and I am reliably informed that similar establishments are to be found throughout Europe and North America.

The next grade up is the local antique dealer whose stock tends to be of early twentieth-century and nineteenth-century artefacts. Such dealers tend not to have a great quantity of furniture, and generally only small chairs and tables, but they often provide a very fruitful hunting ground. After that comes the large, fairly well established antique shop with a stock of furniture, the majority of which will be antique. This is the most likely source for the greater part of the furniture which will appear in the inexpensive category investigated in Part II.

It may well be the case that the proprietor of this type of shop is a member of a professional body, or that a group of local dealers have gathered themselves into an association. Some High Street antique dealers are members of the London and Provincial Antique Dealers' Association (LAPADA). This is probably the second-from-top rank of dealer and members are likely to have much material which is recommended in the upper two categories of Part II.

The pre-eminent antique dealers' association is the British Antique Dealers' Association (BADA) and it is from members' shops that most of the finest antiques generally available in this country are to be had. But the quality can range from some indifferent shops to a handful of the best antique dealers in the world.

The collector should never limit his attentions to any one category of antique shop. A recent classic example, of an antique dealer in a fairly unfashionable part of London selling an important sculpture worth perhaps half a million pounds for only £250, is an extreme but cautionary tale. Another useful type of dealer is a specialist who does not concentrate on furniture, or perhaps the type of furniture you are seeking. For example a dealer in glass may well buy an article such as a small table to sell in his shop, or a specialist dealer in oak might, as a favour to a particular client, purchase a set of mahogany chairs. In such circumstances the collector may well come away with a bargain. So remember, all antique shops are potentially rewarding.

Professional bodies

Some antique dealers regard themselves as professional men in much the same way as a bank manager would. They are holding themselves out as experienced people on whom a prospective purchaser can reply. In order to protect their high reputation the most expert dealers banded together in 1918 to form the British Antique Dealers' Association. Its address is 20 Rutland Gate, London SW7 1BD (01-589 4128). The high standards required of the dealers who have successfully been elected to membership of the organisation ensures its reputation, which has never been seriously challenged. Each year the membership is scrutinised by its committee. There are only about 500 members in Great Britain and most of them specialise to a certain extent, but the great majority do sell good quality furniture. It is for this reason that the buyer of goods from any member of the association can feel confident they they have made a good purchase in the first place and, should there be any grounds for complaint which might emerge later, be reassured by the high professional standards that will be applied. Complaints are properly made to and indeed welcomed by the Council of the association. The association publishes a list of its members which is sent free to those who send a stamped, addressed envelope to the London address. What the association clearly cannot do is to interfere in matters relating to the price of any purchase. Some members are extremely expensive. They themselves would probably not deny this, but they would argue that they are selling works of art which are 'worth it'.

The London and Provincial Antique Dealers' Association (LAPADA) is a similar organisation which embraces a wider spectrum of the trade. Its London address is 112 Brompton Road, London SW3 1JJ (01-584 7911). It includes, in addition to dealers, members who are shippers, restorers, publishers and the like. There is a less rigorous Code of Practice but expertise and experience is required of members. It is, however, more concerned with dealers to the trade, or with the export market, although this is not invariably the case. Some foreign members belong to the association. At present there are about 700 members in total.

Throughout the British Isles there are local associations of antique dealers whose prime purpose is to promote the interests of their members. But it does not follow that membership of such an association on the part of a dealer is to the disadvantage of any member of the buying public. Local organisations have as much need, and desire, to show a high degree of expertise and irreproachable reputation as any Bond Street dealer. Some of the members of local antique dealers' associations are indeed members of both the BADA and LAPADA. Many publish handlists of their members and these can be useful guides during a tour of an area. The two best-known of such associations are the Cotswold Antique Dealers' Association, High Street, Blockley, nr Moreton-in-Marsh, Glos. (038676 280), and the Highland Antique Dealers' Association, Forsyth House, Cromarty, Ross-shire, Scotland. For the sake of completeness it should be recorded that there is an international association of Fine Arts dealers (CINOA) which one seldom comes across in the normal course of events but which promotes internationalism in the field of antiques.

It should not be assumed that a dealer who is not a member of any of the above associations is in any way deficient, or to be discounted. Some dealers go for decorative antiques, indeed some actually practise as interior decorators, and the furniture they sell has great merit. A number of distinguished and long-established interior decorators have an antiques section, and the objects they have for sale are often unusual. Goods from such sources, however, are seldom inexpensive.

How dealers buy

A dealer has to acquire his stock as economically as possible. But he is not very much better equipped than the private buyer as he has few sources that are not available to the individual collector. In effect he has to rely on a greater knowledge of antiques and a greater practical skill in acquiring artefacts. Many dealers ruefully admit that there are plenty of private collectors who have mastered the skills more successfully than the professionals.

FROM THE SALEROOM

The saleroom is one of the principal sources for dealers. They are usually much more experienced in bidding and have a more definite sense of when to stop. The rules of the saleroom apply equally to dealer and private person: both stand before the auctioneer as equals – in theory. One says in theory because there is a practice adopted by small groups of individuals (and the majority of those individuals are dealers) to defraud the vendor of the rightful sale price. This disturbing practice, which is specifically illegal, is called The Ring.

The way in which a ring operates is as follows: a number of individuals agree amongst themselves not to bid against each other at auction. When at the end of the day a number of lots are the property of one or more members of the ring, a second private auction takes place between them. This practice deprives the vendor of his selling price and the auctioneer of a percentage of his commission. An outsider can be squeezed out of the saleroom by the ring specifically bidding against him to prevent his purchase of any lot. The cost of doing this is shared amongst the individual members of the ring. This pernicious practice, although banned by the Auctions (Bidding Agreements) Act of 1927 with penalties attached, carries on in conditions of secrecy. As will be appreciated this type of arrangement is a conspiracy, and conspiracies are notoriously difficult to prove. I have seen the secondary auction taking place on two separate occasions and few knowledgeable dealers, in private, deny that this practice takes place. It seems fair, however, to say that The Ring is less common than it used to be and that local and London auctions attract a far wider group of buyers of varying financial back-up which makes it difficult for the practice to operate effectively and exclusively.

FROM PRIVATE VENDORS

The dealer also buys from private vendors and although it is difficult to assess how much of this goes on, it is reasonable to assume that a fairly high percentage of a dealer's stock will come from such sources. The traditional reason for this is that the vendor often prefers to dispose of property in as discreet a manner as possible. The trade make the point that it is especially worth while selling to a dealer because he does not charge a ten or fifteen per cent commission for selling the goods as an auctioneer will; nor, generally, is the vendor troubled with costs of transport to a saleroom which nowadays are very high. Payment from a dealer is immediate, unlike in salerooms.

What the private vendor should never do is sell to itinerant antique buyers who turn up at doors offering to buy unwanted pieces. Many sensible people and, sadly, many old people have been induced to part with valuables for a fraction of their real worth to these disreputable people. If a sale is wanted, then a local established dealer (or saleroom) is far less risky and almost certainly more profitable.

FROM 'RUNNERS'

Another source from which dealers benefit and which is not really open to the private buyer is the 'runner'. These individuals, or sometimes pairs, travel the country buying up furniture, loading it into the back of a battered old van or a gleaming estate car and taking it round to a number of more-or-less regular dealer buyers. This often explains how a number of craggy old women, seemingly totally immobile, fill their shops continually with attractive antiques which most other dealers cannot find in months of diligent travel. A good and reputable runner (for there are some runners whose sole purpose in life seems to be the disposal of stolen property) is a valuable asset to a dealer.

OTHER SOURCES

Dealers buy from other dealers. Some will only sell to dealers, but the prospective buyer should not be put off by the forbidding 'Trade Only' sign which is really there to discourage time-wasting browsers. A dealer will expect a trade discount on his purchases, which will usually be not less than ten per cent but which is a flexible and negotiable amount. Very few dealers refuse another dealer a trade discount; when they do they are usually specialists in rare areas of collecting, or bloody-minded, or opposed in principle. Often they are a combination of all three.

One way in which a dealer scores over a private buyer is by doing a house 'clearance'. The entire contents will be disposed of for what is usually a small sum. This price reflects the dealer's attitude that he is doing the vendor a favour by taking it all away. A private buyer is in no way able to embark on this method, and indeed only a few dealers are prepared to take on a great deal of worthless rubbish for a few objects of value. (A vendor might be advised, in passing, to remove from sight those objects which are not to be included in the clearance, as they are often used by a dealer as pawns in the negotiation of a price for the clearance.)

Prices at a dealer

When you enter an antique shop you should find that a piece of furniture is described and priced on an attached label. Look on this price as being the highest a dealer hopes to get for it and not what he *expects*. In most cases this will include Value Added Tax, which may be calculated on the ordinary method used in most businesses or on a special scheme whereby tax is payable on a proportion of the selling price. The price may also include the cost of restoration, initial cost, overheads and the infinitely variable profit margin. Occasionally the label will be badly faded, which may indicate that the article has been in the shop for a considerable period of time and is perhaps good value. (There are also other likely explanations.) When the collector gets round to negotiating with a dealer this is all information he should bear in mind.

The trade price that a dealer asks is never marked on a price ticket, except in code, but is more usually decided by the dealer, on consulting his 'book'. Considering that he is usually prepared to make some reduction to a private buyer it is not surprising that he is likely to make an even larger reduction for another dealer, particularly one he knows and regularly trades with. The private buyer can seldom expect to be treated as favourably. There are some dealers who build into their price structure a ten per cent margin which is the trade discount, and others who will work out on a more or less random basis what sort of reduction they are prepared to make, bearing in mind various considerations such as how long the article has been in stock, how likely it is that a future buyer will turn up, subsequent damage to the article since it came into the shop, or even how much he favours the buyer, be he trade or private.

Some dealers do not mark their stock with prices. This is an unsatisfactory course of action which is justified in rare circumstances only. If the stock is appreciating (seldom a serious consideration in furniture) or is unlikely to be sold quickly, or if the dealer is uncertain what price to ask, these are the most usual justifications for the absence of a price. One normally finds that such dealers have in large part a trade clientèle and a wider negotiating range than is usual. But it is recognised that a private buyer is often quite rightly put off by the reluctance of a dealer to quote prices, for he may deduce that the price is tailored to the cut of the customer's clothes. This may not always be so but the inference is understandable. There is one circumstance when a dealer is fair in not lightly disclosing a price and that is in sensitive areas where a high price disclosed might materially affect his sources of supply. This happens at the top end of the market and is, frankly, understandable. Code prices are irresistibly tempting to crack, but they are invariably impossible to solve. They are, however, preferable to having no price displayed at all because the price declared by a dealer is likely to have some foundation in the code.

On the ticket there is normally a description of the article for sale, usually very brief but sufficiently explicit. For example, 'Pair of Regency ebonised armchairs, caned seats, brass enrichments, sabre legs, about 1805'. This is a good description because you do not even need to see the chairs to have a good idea of what they should look like. The description may be less precise, for example, 'Regency chairs, £X the pair'. But such a description does not make a clear representation as to what the chairs are. Sometimes attached to a ticket are the words 'All Faults', or 'As Found', both usually abbreviated to 'AF'. This is supposed to put the apparent and latent defects in the piece within the knowledge of the buyer; it may not in fact have that effect but its appearance on a label does usually indicate some repair or defect.

When a dealer describes a piece of furniture to you take careful note of what he says, and when he writes out a receipt always make him put down in writing exactly what he represented to you. In the event of a subsequent disagreement you will have a description in writing as evidence of the transaction. This is important. If a buyer discovers that the object is not as it was described he may want to take legal action, most particularly under the Misrepresentation Act of 1967, and any evidence of misrepresentation or misdescription will strengthen his case. This does not imply suspicion on the part of the buyer; it is merely the type of care that is essential in the conduct of business affairs.

Negotiating with a dealer

It is most difficult to draw any hard and fast rules as to how to make an offer to a dealer that is lower than the price on the ticket. Clearly you must take the dealer as you find him and rapidly work out the most suitable line of approach. What you must never do is merely pay the price asked for on the ticket (unless it seems so fair that you don't mind paying that amount). A simple question such as, 'Can you do something on this?' or, 'Is there any discount on this?' asked *before* money is shown or a chequebook produced may well have the desired effect. If one is spending, say, £300 on a table a reduction of about £30 is not to be sneered at and may bring the table within one's price range. Asking specifically for a trade price may backfire, particularly when a dealer asks you for your VAT number. An assistant is usually not enabled to offer a discount; in such cases one has to weigh the alternatives of coming back later when the owner is available and of possibly losing the piece for the sake of a few pounds. If one is satisfied that a piece will remain in the shop for some time one might even consider playing a waiting game with the dealer to see if he relents. In most cases one is, alas, doomed to disappointment.

If you are well known to the dealer he might be prepared to allow you time to pay, or the alternative of paying by instalments. Most antique dealers would prefer not to do this but practices of this kind are not unknown in the Fine Art trade where a painting can be paid for by instalments over a couple of months. Certainly the antique trade should examine this method. Part exchange is another way of buying from a dealer but it is neither common nor to the buyer's advantage as a rule. The real difficulty is persuading a dealer to take on something which he would probably not buy in the first place. If one is successful the price for the trade-in piece will not necessarily be realistic.

When discussing a price it is quite in order to point out defects in the hope of getting a reduction in price. If a dealer has not bothered to repair defects – or indeed has not even noticed them – he might be persuaded to make a reduction. But whereas it is quite reasonable to ask for a reduction in the case of ceramics or glass being damaged, most furniture has at some stage or other been repaired or restored to some degree. Perfect examples are rare.

Finally, if you happen to be in a shop when a dealer comes in with some new stock, or if, at an auction sale, you see a dealer with something you have failed to buy but particularly want, there is nothing to stop you offering him a quick profit. The dealer may well refuse, but on the other hand, may be glad to save himself some money on further expenses and liberate his capital (augmented with a small profit) to buy something else. What the dealer is doing is perfectly sensible in business terms and if he sneers at the proposition initially he may come later to rue his rejection of it.

Above all it is important to treat each encounter with a dealer on its merits. The better you know him the easier it will be to negotiate with him. In time you will probably find that you will only go to a small number of dealers whom you have by experience found to be reputable and to sell the kind of stock in which you are interested. But the more dealers you see the more easily you will be able to negotiate with them. You will also see a greater number of antiques. If you show that you have some knowledge of what you are looking for, then often dealers will share their knowledge with you, which can be one of the most effective ways of learning about antique furniture.

SALEROOMS

To buy antiques in a saleroom is exciting, rewarding and risky. As a result it is not suitable for every collector or home furnisher. But for those who can deal with the particular tension of bidding at auction it is well worth while. There are different types of auction and different types of auction house and it may well be that a buyer is a success only at one type. It should not be assumed that all salerooms are conducted on the principles that govern the major London salerooms, Christie's, Sotheby's, Phillips' and Bonham's. Some excellent furniture sales follow on from, and are conducted in about the same manner as, the cattle market. And in between there is an area where the well-heeled rub shoulders with the less well-to-do and both succeed in coming away with bargains.

For those who are fascinated by these things there is a certain psychological interest in the conduct of a sale which is not present when buying from a dealer. To a certain extent we are dealing with a method of collecting which involves a high element of gambling. But if the rules relating to safety are followed properly there is small risk even for the novice. Working out how to bid, or when to bid, when to stop bidding, or when to re-enter bidding – these are all fine points of judgement which will become easier with practice. A potential bidder at auction should spend several sessions sitting at the side of an auction room watching; such a pursuit is in itself an interesting psychological study. It takes longer to master the art of buying at a saleroom if one does not have a natural aptitude. In any case it should only be attempted once you have a knowledge of buying in an antique shop, for there prices can be studied and technical information more easily elicited and accurately grasped than in the frantic rush and tumble of the average sale.

Professional bodies

Auctioneers have two societies which affect the operation of antique sales. First there is the Incorporated Society of Valuers and Auctioneers (ISVA), 3 Cadogan Gate, London SW1 (01-235 2282), which is the main professional association to which auctioneers belong (although membership is by no means compulsory). Its scope covers sale of such things as livestock and real property in addition to antiques and furniture in general. The body which represents Fine Art auctioneers is the Society of Fine Art Auctioneers (SOFA), 7 Blenheim Street, London W1 (01-629 2933) and it seeks to improve the standards of Fine Art aspects of the profession. The membership is not large. The number of salerooms selling what is described as 'antique, secondhand and modern furniture' is very extensive indeed and a useful list of these firms is published in *The British Art & Antiques Yearbook*. It is fair to say that the standard of cataloguing of most small non-specialist auction houses is extremely low and at times is a positive disservice to vendors who have a right to expect some degree of accuracy. It is sad that so few attempts are made to improve matters.

Types of salerooms

SPECIALIST: Main London salerooms and a number of good provincial auction houses do have specialist sales which are accurately catalogued. Of these sales the most common are furniture sales and the better salerooms break down the subject even further into categories such as oak, fine English furniture (by which we mean walnut and mahogany of the eighteenth century and Regency) and Continental. Victorian furniture is similarly treated in a small number of salerooms specialising in this period.

The great advantage is that the lots offered are very accurately described in over ninety-five per cent of the cases and that experts are usually on hand to give opinions in the case of doubt. Lots are for view on one or perhaps two days before the sale. Every lot has an estimated price available for inspection and some catalogues carry printed lists of these prices. Although estimates are not infallible they do serve as a helpful guide in deciding the limit of a bid. On the other hand it is often said that a London saleroom discourages small buyers by its atmosphere. This is partly inevitable, but the buyer should realise that it was only a few years ago that Sotheby's was placing great emphasis on the fact that the majority of lots sold fetched less than £100. This is probably no longer the case, but a goodly percentage still sells for less than £100 and a large number of furniture lots will certainly sell for less than £500.

Specialist salerooms outside London are increasing in number, this being due to a certain extent to the fact that London salerooms are acquiring provincial premises and using them as local headquarters. The standard of cataloguing is high also. These small salerooms frequently have specialist furniture sales, and country house sales which are always worth attending. Apart from the major sales, there are regular auctions to dispose of general accumulated stock. These are excellent sales to attend.

Major salerooms are all coming round to charging a buyer's commission as well as deducting a seller's commission from the knock-down price. At present both of these commissions are charged VAT at the current rate. The rates of commission are about ten per cent but auctioneers have been known, at their discretion, to vary the rates.

LOCAL SALEROOMS

Many local auctioneers have occasional sales of furniture which are usually incidental to their main purpose of selling such items as livestock or agricultural implements, or real property. Small country towns often have a market day when, at the end of the selling of pigs and produce, small groups of furniture are sold off. The prices are usually very low because few dealers attend. These are excellent places to buy old cupboards (for stripping down to the pine), kitchen chairs and tables or even sofas, all of which need cost only a few pounds. You should check to make sure that sofas are not ruined by damp or vermin, for they can stand out in the open market yard for several days covered with an ineffectual tarpaulin. Viewing is usually on the morning of the sale.

Occasionally a good collection of furniture results in a bigger sale. Usually this is in connection with a few house clearances, so that pictures, furniture, glass and ceramics may be mixed up with linen, tin cutlery and garden utensils. Such sales are often very well attended and it should not be assumed that prices will be low. Local dealers attend and it is interesting to note that despite a reasonably affluent private contingent, the dealers usually carry off the trophies.

Small salerooms of this kind do not normally charge a buyer's premium so the only cost that will affect the buyer will be that of carriage back home. This should never be forgotten as carriage can cost more than the lot itself. A wardrobe purchased for ten pounds in a local auction in the Lake District might as well be left on the shores of Lake Windermere rather than be transported to some London suburb.

The view

Buy a catalogue and view the goods properly. Do not merely glance, but peer inside, underneath, wherever, to check for defects. One of the reasons why furniture is put into a sale is because something is wrong with it. Some people, for fear of revealing a specific interest, will diligently examine everything except the lot they are hoping to buy. The consequences are self-evident. Porters at auctions usually have some useful information to impart, and since they often have commissions to bid for absent buyers, will be able to give a good idea of the estimate (country sales seldom have estimates). In Chapter 3, the section headed 'What to look for' on page 30 gives an idea of what the buyer should scrutinise, pointing out the normal types of defect we associate with, say, a dresser, or a Windsor chair. The point about a view is this: if a buyer has been afforded the opportunity to examine all the lots for a reasonable period of time he is deemed to be aware of the normal defects that are detectable on inspection. The rule of *caveat emptor*, or let the buyer beware, is particularly relevant to the world of auction sales.

Reserves

A seller who wishes to protect his property from being knocked down for a laughable sum will impose a reserve, usually with the auctioneer's advice but sometimes independently. This is very common in the case of London salerooms; much less so in the country. Broadly speaking the buyer should always assume a reserve exists. During bidding the auctioneer will take a bid 'from the chandelier' until the reserve is reached, and if no bidding continues he will withdraw the lot.

Bidding

It is important to make yourself known to the auctioneer if you propose to make a bid as he may feel that he needs assurances as to your credit worthiness. This is usually a mere formality. It is sensible to introduce yourself at least to his clerk so that he will be watching for your bid. Having decided what sum to go to, try not to become carried away.

Make your bid clearly and deliberately and keep your hand raised until the auctioneer sees it; shout if he doesn't. It may happen that you are the only person interested in that lot. The auctioneer will start off by suggesting a sum which may be the reserve, but there is no reason why you should not call out a lesser sum, perhaps half the lowest sum suggested by the auctioneer. Sometimes the point at which you join the bidding is critical, for if you have set yourself a limit you may have to bid over that by the unfortunate chance of your opponent bidding this exact sum. You might then decide to offer a pound or so more, thereby only marginally exceeding your limit. The auctioneer may not accept this bid if the increase is derisory but in most cases he will.

If you feel uncertain of your own ability in bidding you can place your bid with the auctioneer, with a porter, or indeed you can ask anybody to bid on your behalf. But then there is a slight risk that a bidder will bid you up to the top of your limit, so if possible it seems better to bid personally.

Having placed your bid and succeeded, payment falls due immediately or within the terms of the auction house rules, usually printed in the catalogue. Usually you may not remove your purchases until the sale is ended and the auctioneer has indicated satisfaction with your method of payment. Always collect your goods as soon as possible. There is a high risk of damage and if your purchase is very valuable you should ask the auctioneer about temporary insurance cover. After a period of time uncollected lots are put into store and the buyer is charged money accordingly.

Disadvantages

The rule of *caveat emptor* (let the buyer beware) is fairly undiluted in auction sales.
Latent defects may well be the responsibility of the buyer.
It is difficult to view in some circumstances.
The speed of an auction sale can disadvantage a buyer by pressurising him into buying at the wrong price or not buying at all.
The buyer may in some cases have to pay a commission to the auctioneer.

Advantages

A saleroom is often cheaper than a dealer, despite a buyer's commission.
The price reached is competitive and is seen to be so.
Restoration usually has yet to be done so the buyer can supervise this personally.

ANTIQUE MARKETS AND FAIRS

Market stallholders should be considered separately from dealers with their own premises.

Permanent sites

In London and the provinces there are associations of dealers of all kinds who rent stalls in covered buildings and operate from them as though they were operating from a shop. Many of these dealers are most distinguished; some are members of BADA. In some cases the dealers themselves select other dealers who wish to join them. But other markets are less reputable and stable. It is for this reason that there is still a slight element of risk in buying from some markets. Fortunately, because furniture is not the easiest commodity in a midnight flit, dealers in furniture are often the most stable members of a covered market. On the other hand, space is seldom vast and dealers are more likely to concentrate on small furniture. In London there are a number of highly reputable markets, in the fairly high price range. In the major antique centres of England there are good markets, notably in Bath, Cheltenham, Edinburgh, Warwick and the more elegant of our country towns and local centres.

Street markets

Much has been written in favour of street markets. The Portobello Road market is the most famous of its kind in the world. Furniture is not ideally traded in such situations although it does happen. Cheaper and usually smallish pieces turn up. In many of these street markets, Portobello and Bermondsey in particular, stolen goods can be passed on to the public, who in certain circumstances can acquire a good title in them.

There are good and bad times to visit street markets. First, find out when the market is open as times are very rigid. Go early, for example before 6 a.m. at Bermondsey and before 9 a.m. on the Portobello Road. These are the times when the dealers are around buying from the stall holders. Go also when everybody is packing up to leave, for last minute reductions are made, particularly with bulky objects. It must be said that the street markets are only rewarding when cheap furniture is sought. The better pieces come up for sale in different ways.

Antique fairs

Some antique fairs represent the best and some the worst ends of the market. They certainly underline the vast interest in collecting shown by all groups of society.

The most prestigious, the Burlington House Antiques Fair (with luck only temporarily in abeyance), takes place in London annually in June. The furniture displayed runs into millions of pounds worth and most of the best dealers in the country have stands. It is self-regulatory, but notwithstanding, the quality is unimpeachable. Most people interested in antiques visit the fair; few buy, but they are only inhibited by financial considerations. All over Great Britain and also in Europe important fairs take place regularly. In England the major fairs are at Olympia (June), Harrogate (September), Solihull (March), Bath (September), Chelsea (December and May) and Camden (July). From the point of view of the buyer these fairs are never cheap but the quality of the pieces is extremely high. Unfortunately these popular events are crowded and it is often difficult to see what you are looking for.

Below this level there is an increasing number of collectors' fairs, normally of one day's duration, which take place on Sundays in large hotels or convenient meeting halls. The best way to find out when these fairs take place is to look in the *What's On* page of the weekend supplement of your local newspaper. Most of these fairs deal in small collectables but sometimes furniture is for sale.

BUYING PRIVATELY

Private advertisements appear in most newspapers offering antique furniture for sale. (Sometimes dealers, masquerading as private vendors, advertise similarly.) Providing the buyer has confidence in his own judgement and is satisfied about the price, this can be a good means of acquiring furniture. But it is difficult at times to say no. Also, although it is difficult to be categorical, a vendor normally asks fairly high prices for antique furniture, for his scheme is really to avoid a middleman (in other words a dealer or auctioneer). This method of buying is best done with a fairly good idea of the current state of prices in addition to an awareness of likely defects. Some advertisements in antique journals are worth investigation but again they are not the cheapest place to buy. The advertiser has probably gleaned comparable prices from the magazine.

The risk about buying privately is that a mistake cannot with ease be rectified. The vendor seldom holds himself out as an expert so it is unreasonable for the buyer to rely on any technical description. This type of purchase should be carefully considered.

THE SKIP

Some furniture, even antique furniture, is acquired free from a roadside skip or the corporation tip. It appears to be illegal to do so, even if for the most altruistic of motives. So this book cannot recommend it: leave it to the corporation dustmen.

3
Is It a Fake?

THE biggest fear the ordinary man will have when he has ventured into the field of buying antique furniture is that of buying a fake. Apart from the (mistaken) impression that antique furniture is more expensive than modern, it is fear of fakes that may have driven him away from buying antiques. It is very odd, then, that when a potential collector does turn away from antiques he frequently turns instead to reproduction furniture, most of which is a thoroughly depressing alternative as well as being a species of the kind of thing he was initially afraid of buying.

Of course it is an excellent aim to acquire sufficient specialist knowledge to avoid buying a fake, even if you have adequate funds to buy in the kind of antique shop where fakes are thought not to exist. The section 'What to look for' on page 30 outlines the areas where fakes give themselves away. It is almost impossible for a fake to be one hundred per cent convincing but this is small consolation to the collector who because of gaps in his own knowledge is persuaded to buy a spurious example.

Fakes have been made for many generations and one could take the point of view that this practice is an honest attempt to imitate the fine production of the past. The fact that in most cases corners are cut leads us to deduce that commercial gain has been the real driving force, not an attempt to honour the past. Fakes start to appear as soon as collectors appear; there are seventeenth- and eighteenth-century examples of men driven by a collecting mania whose enthusiasm blinded them to defects. But it was in the nineteenth century that fakes began to appear with a solid regularity, aiming to trap collectors as a class and not as individuals. It was easy to take people in because historical research, into furniture in particular, was underdeveloped. Historical fakes include a large number of spurious versions of the 'Saxon' chair in Warwick Almshouses; and there was a group of reproductions which widely popularised the style. But the so-called 'Saxon' chair was in fact a turned chair probably of the seventeenth century.

CONSEQUENCES OF BUYING A FAKE

First and foremost, the reputation of the seller will be diminished, whether he is a dealer, auctioneer or any other vendor. (This assumes the dealer has made no representations as to any material defect, indicating that it was essentially a period piece.) The proper course for the buyer in these circumstances is to return it to the dealer. It is not essentially what he contracted to buy and a reputable dealer, in particular one who is a member of an antique dealers' association, is likely to accept responsibility and take back the piece, refunding the money in whole. Possibly, with the purchaser's consent, the dealer will replace the spurious piece with a genuine one of the same description or an article of equal value. If he refuses, the dealer can be reported to his association, if he has one, or if that fails the buyer may feel inclined to have recourse to legal process and remedy. A sharp letter from a solicitor usually brings matters to a swift conclusion. As was said in

Chapter 2 it all depends on the dealer being prepared to accept that what he sold was in fact described by him as genuine. The reader will see the clear importance of having a precise documentary description made by the dealer or his assistant at the time the object is purchased. If there is no evidence available other than word of mouth the buyer is, to use a cricketing term, on a sticky wicket.

When inexpensive furniture is purchased a dealer does not always make clear representations. This is usually because it is not always the custom to give this kind of description, or perhaps some restoration has altered the nature of a piece of furniture, or the dealer simply does not have the knowledge. It is unlikely in these circumstances that a dealer will be persuaded to take anything back if he does not want to.

Salerooms would normally be in exactly the same position as dealers were they materially to misdescribe furniture, but always scrutinise the conditions of sale printed in the front of the catalogue. It sometimes happens that defects which are not complained of within a specified period may well have to go by the board.

In short, the collector who buys a fake and is unable to come to terms with the seller will experience some financial loss. In the case of an expensive antique this may be very considerable indeed; perhaps many thousands of pounds. Luckily, bad cases of this kind are rare. Lesser cases, where the object purchased may have a value of only a hundred pounds or so, are more usual and it has to be said that this is one of the unavoidable hazards of collecting. The great value of such a mishap is that the collector learns more from it than he does from considerable study. It sharpens his perceptions and quickens his suspicions, so that provided he is not disheartened (and there is no reason why he should be as every great collector has made blunders in the early stages) he is better equipped to carry on collecting. This is not just vain enthusiasm; it has often been shown to be the case. So the collector is left with a dud, which he can move out of the way if he wants, but as he no doubt bought it for reasons and needs which still exist he may prefer to keep it in the place for which it was originally intended.

WHEN A RESTORED PIECE BECOMES A FAKE

Wild restoration can have disastrous consequences for an antique: it should always be contemplated with discretion. Chapter 4 looks more thoroughly at problems besetting restorers. It is difficult to draw clear lines as to when repairs change the nature of an antique so thoroughly that it ceases to be an antique – to the extent that it is a positive untruth to describe it as such. But the effect on the value of the piece is very considerable indeed. Unlike most other collectables, furniture is more usually improved in value by being sensibly restored, whereas restoration to, say, china nearly always ruins it as a collector's piece and relegates it to the level of being merely decorative. But even with furniture, there are those who would say that, regardless of value, an excessively restored piece ceases even to be decorative.

Take a classic example, typical of many. Some years ago a well known dealer restorer (whose reputation for quality far exceeds his slightly questionable renown for restoration) was sent a good eighteenth-century Italian painted commode for repairs to the extensively damaged paintwork. The paintwork could certainly have been touched up, arduously but satisfactorily. What in fact happened was that the dealer stripped and repainted the whole commode, albeit with such skill that only the most expert eye could distinguish the finished work from what should have been the result, and the owner could certainly detect no discrepancy. It should be clear that to describe such an example as being eighteenth-century when all that was visible was modern (apart from the form) was stretching the truth unreasonably. Similar and common cases are when a bureau, for example, has been completely reveneered. There are more examples of this type of 'restoration' than you may think.

IS IT SENSIBLE TO BUY A FAKE?

Given that a heavily restored piece of furniture is not the best type to buy, what are the general rules relating to when and when not to make a purchase. There are no hard and fast rules. Each example has to be judged on its merits and there are inevitable problems relating to personal taste. The collector of first-rate examples will be more demanding; clearly a pristine example is most to be sought, though these are rare. Nearly all furniture has at some stage or other experienced some minor repairs and the average householder endeavouring to furnish his home may be prepared to take a less uncompromising approach.

The British Antique Dealers' Association gives recommendations as to the extent of restoration beyond which a piece of furniture will be ineligible for an antiques fair (although this may not be a buyer's prime consideration). Chairs, for example, frequently have weakened joints and you would expect these to be properly strengthened. Legs, particularly on country chairs, have often worn down, are worm-eaten or have decayed for other reasons, and individual members may have been replaced. Stretchers and backsplats are also very commonly replaced. Upholstery is almost always replaced but original upholstery should be preserved if it is both antique and in good enough condition. Seventeenth- and early eighteenth-century embroidered upholstery to wing chairs of the same period is a great enhancement of their value if properly restored.

As has been indicated in the previous section some restoration to painted furniture is permissible, but frequently examples are completely repainted because half a job inexpertly done looks unattractively uneven. This may well be a case of indifferent and undesirable restoration; even the most skilled restorers are sometimes unable to reproduce the surface of some pieces that have aged in a particularly distinctive way. If you choose to buy painted furniture ask a dealer about the extent to which it has been restored. A gilt mirror on the other hand is often completely regilded, and discoloured glass is replaced with modern or reproduction glass. Such drastic restoration if properly done only increases the value. It is clear that there are areas of inconsistency.

The aim of the collector restorer should be this: to conserve the original features wherever possible. A dealer looks at things slightly differently, realising that by losing some original features he is making the antique look much more saleable. The aim of the buyer should be to judge between the alternatives and exercise his own taste, bearing in mind the purpose for which he is buying the piece and perhaps being prepared in some cases to sacrifice absolute genuineness for usefulness.

TWO TYPES OF 'FAKE'

Reproductions

In one sense a reproduction is not a fake at all as it does not seek to deceive the buyer; it stands before you without attempting to deny the period in which it was made. Reproductions are not just things of the recent past. They were being made in the nineteenth century; many chairs which appear to be Chippendale period were in fact made in the later years of the nineteenth century using good wood and identical methods of manufacture. Sometimes the proportions are not true, but this is the only difference between these reproductions and the eighteenth-century versions. Even the evidence of age is there, and genuine age, for the reproduction chairs may have been in continuous use from the date they were made and show signs of wear which are entirely consistent with the marks on a period Chippendale chair. These chairs, although reproduction, are now thought to be a proper concern of furniture historians of the late nineteenth century and not merely an unimportant aberration.

So today reproductions are also made. The timbers and cheap production that were available only a few years ago are no longer easily obtained, so the manufacturers, faced with a very considerable demand, maintain the styles (sometimes slightly simplified) and economise on materials and use slightly more machine work. In effect these are low-grade manufacturers, better avoided except for the odd purchase. A set of dining chairs is not less expensive than some period furniture of greater originality in design. The use of mahogany veneers persists, but it is thin veneer protected by thick, lustrous varnish. Legs and stretchers are seldom in mahogany at the lower end of the market but more often of a cheaper wood stained to a tone which matches the mahogany veneers but can be easily detected on close examination.

There are, however, reproductions which are of very high quality indeed. The firms who make these pieces reproduce furniture in the orthodox traditions of good cabinet making. A Queen Anne-style bureau made by these craftsmen can cost £10,000, at a time when a good quality period example can cost £25,000. It is generally agreed that these will not appreciate in the same way as genuine antiques, but it is very questionable exactly what they will do from the point of view of value. Traditionally reproductions lose their value at first. It is likely that these high quality reproductions will do the same initially but in the long term will appreciate in value. One or two firms have now started up who make very high quality reproduction furniture but not by the same techniques as the cabinet makers referred to above and the craftsmen of old. Chipboard, blockboard and laminated woods are used for carcass material, for the simple reason that the central heating of today damages old wood by the fluctuations in humidity it causes. Blockboard, for example, is less prone to these damaging influences. These pieces of furniture are also expensive; a late Georgian-style breakfast table can cost £800 when its period equivalent can cost between £1,500 and £2,000.

So although modern reproduction furniture is not really within the scope of this book, some examples of fairly good quality are being made and one should dutifully refer to their existence. Cheap reproductions are not really good value compared to genuine period furniture which is available for the same price providing that you are prepared to make the effort to look for it.

Marriages

A marriage describes a recognisable piece of furniture made up from an amalgamation of two other separate pieces of furniture. Both pieces may be absolutely original. The ultimate aim is that the finished product is more likely to command a higher price than the combined prices of the two originals. Here are five examples:

(a) The bureau bookcase is much more expensive than a bureau on its own; perhaps twice or three times as much for a good example. So a bureau is matched up with a cabinet or a bookcase and the result is often convincing. The veneers on the side should be checked; the age of the backboards should be considered; the carcass woods to both top and bottom should be compared; the proportions should be closely looked at as this is often the first visible giveaway; and the top of the bureau should be scrutinised for evidence of alteration. As a fine bureau bookcase can cost between £2,500 and £30,000 and upwards, the buyer should take advice if he is not confident – and probably even if he is.

(b) A pedestal dining table is expensive and large examples are even more so. So the top of one table is often married with the base of another. A tripod table with a tip top is utilised (the sturdier the better) and an old top of a cheap Victorian mahogany table or merely some old timber is enlisted. Matching pedestals are often used when they are available but in some cases the need for an exact match is dispensed with. The shape of furniture of this kind nearly always gives it away. The bases are usually too flimsy and the timber used to unite the base with the top is frequently modern.

It is more difficult to spot a marriage when the genuine base to a dining table is combined with the genuine top of another dining table, both being of the same period and style. The timber will probably differ slightly, giving the buyer a clue, and the proportions may disclose the fraud, although rather subtly. Always examine the means whereby the top is affixed to the base for suspicious signs.

(c) An early Victorian or Georgian pole screen is often used with a circular wooden top (sometimes a small, pie crust edged tray) to make a wine table, often called a candle stand. They are distinguishable from the originals (which are very expensive and rare) by the spindly proportions at the top part of the stem.

(d) A George II dining chair of good wide proportions is sometimes fitted with arms from another chair so as to increase its value. The seat of a genuine example will be of more expansive proportions. Such a chair was recently rejected from a major London antique fair though it looked outstandingly convincing.

(e) Queen Anne period cabinets on stands are often marriages. In these cases the proportions and, more generally, the state of the veneer and the carcass give the game away. Genuine examples cost between £3,000 and £30,000 and upwards.

We may deduce that the buying of marriages cannot be recommended except when the drawbacks have been pointed out. First of all, even when both parts of the marriage are perfectly genuine and above reproach, perhaps even free of all restoration, the marriage itself is not a genuine antique. This is a purist's view and is a little difficult to maintain if the marriage was effected only a short time after the individual pieces were made. Secondly, the marriage cannot increase in value at the same rate or to the same extent as an original specimen, although the increase in value may be perfectly satisfactory and may even overtake the rate of inflation. But all this is said in the light of the facts that marriages are often extremely easy on the eye, fit with remarkable ease into modern and period interiors and, more important, are within the pocket of a wider range of collectors than the originals. So although no recommendation is made, neither is any discouragement given.

WHAT TO LOOK FOR

In an antique shop or at a view in an auction room, endeavour to examine furniture for signs of repairs, or in an extreme case evidence of a complete forgery. The following is a discussion of structural and stylistic aspects which are of some assistance in finding out the state of the furniture offered for sale.

Proportions

A fake or a copy of a period chair does not usually have the same proportions as an original. Take a mid-Georgian dining chair. These chairs usually have very generous proportions and in particular a wide seat. Fakes and reproductions do not usually have such wide seats and the difference can be as much as five or six inches. This is not conclusive evidence but a useful fact to use in conjunction with others.

The height of a seat can indicate that the chair has been cut down (do not forget that 'nursing' chairs have low seats). Semicircular side tables of the Sheraton period have often been cut down by a few inches when, for example, a castor has broken (it is easier to cut off all the castors than to repair them). As a very general principle, table tops for eating off or writing on are about 74 cm (29 in) off the ground; if there is any wide discrepancy something might be amiss.

All this is measured not so much in centimetres or inches but in the loss of proportion with which the furniture started off life. The more you read books and look at illustrations of period furniture the more you will become aware of good proportions. One of the most typical ways in which a student or an expert in furniture expresses his doubts about a piece is in the words, 'It doesn't look quite right.'

Legs

Legs are often replaced as they usually have to bear great weights and endure oblique strains and stresses so they wear out or weaken at the joints.

(a) In case a chair or table leg has been replaced, or in fact any other leg to a piece of furniture, you should first check to see if all legs are of the same wood. Only in the case of country furniture is there any chance that they will genuinely be different. The wood of a replaced leg will have been stained to make it the same colour as the other legs but the figure and grain will normally be sufficiently distinct to enable it to be detected.

(b) Legs should all have the same quality of carving; one that is too sharply carved may well be a replacement.

(c) Signs of wear should be consistent with wear on the other legs. The practice of simulating the marks of age is known as 'distressing'. What usually happens is that the distresser strikes the leg with various hard implements (typically chains) to give some signs of wear. But seldom are those signs truly consistent.

(d) Some chair legs have been carved up to make them more ornate. The classic instance of this is the George II chair with cabriole legs carved at the knees with foliage or lion's-head masks. The procedure for checking such examples is to look at the profile of the cabriole leg and to check on the depth of the carving; if it is shallow there is some chance that the carving has been added at a later date.

(e) Some legs which have broken through have been repaired. Normally the joint is visible where there has been a straight joining and this is often a dangerous weakness and indication of a deficient repair. Sometimes a new half leg has been recarved and replaced and if the repair is clean this is likely to be a stronger method.

(f) Joints at the top of the leg are often braced. This is a precaution and is often done to increase the life of the chair. It is not evidence of widespread restoration.

(g) Look for signs of genuine patination (although most antique furniture has in fact lost its patination). As a chair wears through use so also does it take on colour and depth of polish. Artificial patination is more even than patination born of years of care. A single leg sometimes shows a different patina to any other and this should be looked on with suspicion.

Feet

Feet have been in contact with the ground as well as having had to take the downward strain of a chair and endure the friction and vibration of continuous movement. So worm and dampness can quickly consume the wood, while movement abrades it. You should assume that the older and larger the furniture the more likely it is that the feet have been replaced. In the second half of the eighteenth century, brass castors on the legs of tables (and some chairs) reduced the damage done by dragging them across the floor. Brass castors are usually original but leather runners on some will have been replaced.

(a) Bun feet and block feet have usually been replaced. Chests of drawers and larger structures before about 1710 stood mainly on bun feet, and oak furniture of earlier times had simple blocks which were an extension of the carcass. It is very unusual for a bun foot to be original as they were not always of oak but also of pine, so in addition to rotting were susceptible to worm. Such repairs are in order, and fine specimens of furniture at Burlington House Antiques Fair have been known to have had bun feet replaced.

(b) Bracket feet on chests of drawers seldom survive undamaged because pulling the chests across the floor will have put the feet under a strain for which they were not intended. Bracket feet are often reinforced with a square block behind them. Unfortunately this again is usually of pine which is eaten by worm and drops off, so the feet become fundamentally weakened. Veneer on bracket feet is very often replaced. Again these repairs, even an entire replacement of the bracket feet, are acceptable to most collectors.

(c) Cabriole legs of the squat variety, and the delicate French counterpart *pieds de biche*, are frequently worn. A French armoire, or wardrobe, often has *pieds de biche* feet which are part of the massive structure of the piece but carved into their elegant shape. Restoration is often very complicated in situations where such legs have gone; it is always difficult to get carving done satisfactorily nowadays. The extremities of many of these feet – the pads, or the toes or claws – are frequently broken and have been repaired. These repairs are in order providing they are well done. Glueing is seldom adequate.

(d) Big splits in feet and legs are dangerous and can worsen. A bad split is difficult to repair adequately.

(e) Brass fittings are usually original but it is always desirable to check (see page 34).

Stretchers and rails

As with legs and feet, stretchers and rails are structural and the continued strains to which they are put make them casualties in the knockabout of ordinary life. Stretchers in particular are not always strong in themselves, but they impart a strength to the overall structure which is crucial. When a stretcher is broken on a dining room chair many people do not replace it as it appears so flimsy that they are led to believe its need must have been negligible. In fact the chair is very soon badly weakened and the owner may have to expend greater sums of money in repairing loose joints. Rails, that is seat rails and cresting rails, are essentially structural and the loss of either makes a chair useless. Seat rails do not often break, except for some reason on country chairs, when iron braces are often found serving as a good if conspicuous repair. Cresting rails *do* break, especially on high-backed chairs, and urgent repairs are required. Usually any repair of this kind is clearly visible, or a hand gently drawn over the surface alerts the buyer by a passing roughness or change in texture. As a general principle, a buyer should pass his fingertips over the furniture and not rely on the evidence of his eyes alone.

(a) With the usual exception in the case of country furniture check and see if the stretcher is of the same kind of wood as the rest of the chair.

(b) If a stretcher is turned, see if the turning matches the turning on other stretchers, and if there are any sharp grooves.

(c) Look for signs of wear in the right places. Stretchers are often bruised or distressed without regard to what is a likely form of wear. On a desk or bureau, for instance, wear will probably only be visible on the stretcher on which generations of feet have been propped.

(d) Inside a seat rail look to see if the colour of the wood is even. Seldom are rails repaired with old wood, though often it is stained to represent an even appearance.

(e) Old seat rails should have evidence of earlier upholstery or old railing, and it is difficult to imitate nail marks.

(f) Similarly worm holes which are evident on some rails or stretchers but which are absent on others may indicate some replacements. Worm holes are faked on more expensive pieces but not at all on cheaper restorations.

Upholstery

Old furniture has generally lost its upholstery. When it does survive in good or restorable condition it increases the value of the furniture considerably, although there are many dealers who readily admit that old upholstery does not automatically increase saleability. A dealer may claim that upholstery is original, for instance on a stool. The stool may be eighteenth-century and the upholstery may also be eighteenth-century but there is seldom a good reason for assuming they started out life together. The better evidence is the stuffing and technique of upholstery underneath the cover. If it is visible you should examine it as far as you can. Some stools have black cloth pinned underneath the chair to prevent sight of the stuffing, but this is normally confined to examples dating from 1830 and later.

Upholstery may conceal considerable restoration, especially as totally upholstered furniture is often made of beech which is especially prone to worm. Unfortunately the eye cannot discern such work and the buyer should question the dealer.

Interior-sprung upholstery dates from about 1830 and it often has to be renewed.

When the buyer sees a sofa in need of restoration he should realise that such work is very expensive indeed. It can cost well over £150 to have a five pound armchair properly restored.

Expensive furniture covered with non-contemporary, very expensive textiles should be avoided. Resale will not adequately take into account the cost of the textile. Foam rubber stuffing and synthetic velvet are not period features and are unattractive in antique furniture. Avoid them at all costs.

Veneers: not always what they seem

Old veneer has been replaced and faked throughout this century and well into the last. It is difficult to do it nowadays but there are skilled restorers and fakers who are capable of cutting veneer in exactly the same way as in the late seventeenth century. Fine repairs and fakes are in fact often very difficult to detect. There is, however, a difference in thickness, the early veneers being 0.1–0.3 cm ($\frac{1}{16}$–$\frac{1}{8}$in) thick and later machine-cut veneers being as much as six times as thin (and thinner, one now hears).

Many chests of drawers and other examples of veneered furniture have had minor repairs, as the thin veneer is very prone to flake off at vulnerable points, and these minor replacements are often visible. This is quite in order and very common. What is unacceptable is when an entire surface has been reveneered. Old walnut, when laid on to the top of a table or a chest of drawers, was most usually quarter-veneered, with matched quarters covering the surface. Later tops do not have this feature.

Always attempt to see how thick the veneer is by means such as looking at the back or examining the inside of drawers; it is a very good guide to age. Minor repairs can be done yourself if the furniture is not too valuable but extensive work should be done by an expert who will, alas, be expensive.

Paintwork

Paintwork has been referred to previously (see page 26). Some furniture has been overpainted with a cheap paint, covering either good wood (fairly unusual) or earlier painting. Normally an inspection of a piece offered for sale will reveal some chipped surface that will yield clues. Some mirrors, chairs, and a few other pieces of furniture have been painted over a gesso base (gesso is a form of plaster of paris) and restoration work is difficult in these instances.

Always make sure the paintwork is as little restored as possible. Tôle, a form of painted, tinned sheet iron, has often rusted underneath, and repairs are usually of the kind that rip off all the surface paint, leaving it decorative but from the purist's point of view worthless. Restorative paintwork is normally visible. Do not assume that Victorian pine chests of drawers were overpainted long after they were made. Much paintwork is original and should be retained if possible.

Looking glasses

Old glass, that is glass of the seventeenth and eighteenth centuries, is extremely thin and the silvering on the back is highly susceptible to damage, particularly by damp. If in bad condition it discolours and flakes off and in extreme cases it is impossible to see your face in the glass. If you take a point of a pencil you can check on the thickness of the glass which will give some indication of its age. The surface of old glass will also reflect with some unevenness. Nineteenth-century glass is much thicker and heavier but is also capable of being damaged and gravely discoloured by the damp.

A modern glass has been developed which has the appearance of old eighteenth-century glass. In other words it is slightly distorted, whereas modern floatglass in commercial production is lifelessly perfect. Many old mirrors have had glass replaced which is a commercial recognition on the part of dealers that tarnished looking glasses do not sell except to period perfectionists. For gilded mirrors, see the next section.

Gilding

As with looking glasses, upholstery and paintwork, too decayed an original condition has the effect of deterring buyers. A badly damaged gilt frame normally has to be regilded in order to be resaleable. There are two types of gilding, water and oil, the first usually bright and the second duller. Today nearly all gilding is of the water variety.

Damage to gilding is normally evident by white plaster being exposed, but sometimes it has been disastrously 'touched up' by amateurs with a gold paint which is not actually gold and has a tone which clashes with original gilding. The extent of the damage should be taken into consideration; it should be said that regilding is highly expensive so a buyer should consider carefully before he buys a piece that will need extensive restoration.

Brasswork

Most brass handles and keyholes are not original to the piece of furniture to which they are affixed and most are not period at all when we come to look at early eighteenth-century handles or before. Stylistically it is usually easy to identify most handles to within a decade or so. But it is fatal to attempt to date a piece of furniture on the evidence of brasswork.

In the nineteenth century brass handles were unfashionable and in many cases were replaced with turned wooden handles. The evidence of this alteration having been carried out and then renewed (using non-period brass) will be minor repairs to the veneer where the changes took place and holes on the inside of a drawer. Always look out for signs of wear (an indication of old brass), and check to see how well brass 'sits' on a drawer.

Often brass finials have been replaced or added. Usually the replacements are modern reproductions, sometimes individually cast from one survivor. They can deceive, especially if the restorer rechisels the finial after casting to produce a better finish.

Stability

Do not forget in this frantic concern for suspect features that if you are buying furniture to sit on, or eat off, or make use of in some other way, there is an aspect sometimes more important than genuineness; the furniture should be capable of carrying out the function for which it was intended or for which you intend to use it. So always remember that a table must be stable, that chairs made for a bedroom may not bear the weight of a diner, regardless of how attractive they may look, and that some desks have remarkably low kneeholes making it difficult to sit comfortably. These are all matters for common sense rather than for being set down in a list, but you should not forget them. Scholars often do, but there is no reason why you should.

4
Restoration and Conservation

ALTHOUGH it is a cardinal argument in this book that antique furniture is as robust, if not more so, than modern it has to be admitted that in the course of time some damage will be experienced by a high proportion of examples. So the problem of restoration has to be considered thoroughly.

In museums restoration is a vexed question: has so-and-so gone too far in repairing that cabinet; is the upholstery to that sofa absolutely accurate? Much effort is expended in researching minor points. In the world of general antiques, although the aim is to be as historically and technically accurate as possible, the real test is one of taste and reasonableness. Recently the question of economy has also been added to these practical considerations and this always tempts people into the area of do-it-yourself. In many cases common sense should dissuade the amateur repairer from embarking on any course of restoration which is beyond his abilities. If you do have a piece of antique furniture in good condition, restored or otherwise, there is an additional problem of how to maintain this condition, preserving it from the risk of deterioration that modern life can bring to antiques.

THE COST OF RESTORATION

Alas, inflation has greatly increased the cost of restoration, particularly in respect of the raw materials required. It is said that the number of restorers has diminished. Though this may well have been true in the past twenty years, a number of technical courses have produced a new generation of young and competent restorers. This new generation is probably more professional than the old school, but is not cheap. A cheap restorer is usually not a good restorer; it is always hard to preach on the vice of false economy but there seems to be little doubt that in respect of furniture it breeds a great deal of difficulty later. It is not intended in this section to quantify the cost of restoration as there is no recognised scale. Whereas a Regency armchair of about 1805 of the Trafalgar type and of good quality would be fairly certain to cost about £200–£300, if it were badly damaged, one restorer might quote quite a different price from another. The number of man-hours required can explain why one small repair is charged for at a different rate to another superficially similar repair. Restorers are notoriously slow and good ones use their own time scale.

Upholstery

Reupholstery is not especially expensive as the skill is not great (see page 37 for advice on home upholstery). But the textiles used can vary enormously in quality and price. Restoration of old textiles is a much more skilled job. They may require cleaning, or the restoration of appliqué work or embroidery, and these tasks when done by an expert can take a great deal of time.

Rejointing chairs

Although not highly skilled this is an arduous job and is best entrusted to an expert. It is expensive. A set of chairs can take up a great deal of time so a restorer will normally take them on in ones and twos. Unless you are satisfied that he will not bore holes in the limbs and apply plastic wood indiscriminately, do not rely on a local craftsman to do this work.

Replacing broken members

Luckily, broken members of chairs tend to be stretchers and backsplats (or parts of backs). When the only task for the restorer is turning a new stretcher on a lathe or cutting a stretcher of straightforward square shape this is not especially expensive. Damage to the carved backs of chairs can, however, be very expensive to repair.

Stripping furniture

Commercial specialists in stripping have a tariff for certain common articles of furniture such as wardrobes, chests of drawers and chairs. But this type of stripping in large baths of caustic soda is not to be recommended for good antiques and the usual way is bit by bit with a paint stripper, which can be more easily controlled. This second method is more expensive because much more time is required; it should, however, be within the capabilities of the amateur restorer. Removing paint with wire wool is a more arduous course still but providing care is taken the owner can also do this himself. The final method applies to expensive furniture which has been overpainted; it is the expensive (because laborious) course of 'dry cleaning', flaking off coats of paint to reveal an original painted surface or overpainted patina.

Touching up paintwork

In the hands of an expert restorer this can be moderately expensive. It is a different skill from that of cabinet making, and specialist restorers of this kind are few and far between and appear to be very busy. Simple jobs can be carried out at home (see page 38).

Veneering

This can be the most expensive course of restoration of all, especially when complex inlay and marquetry need attention. The services of an expert are essential; it is not the kind of work that even your local dealer's 'little man' can be allowed to do. Simple work may, however, be entrusted to him with a good deal of safety, for example replacing small pieces of veneer from drawers or repairing damaged crossbanding or stringing.

Repolishing

This is a job that the owner can usually do himself, but if the aim is to build up a depth and colour of polish in a short time it is backbreaking work. French polishing is best left to an expert; this is fairly expensive but worth while. For information on polishes, see page 42.

Gilding

Gilding, which uses real gold leaf not cheap gold paint, is extremely skilled and expensive. There are relatively few good gilders. A carved frame or a good chair will need expert attention and take a good deal of time. Inexpensive items can be dealt with by students of gilding but, it cannot be repeated enough, **leave your good gilding to the experts.**

The cost of restoration is going to be less high to a dealer, especially as he frequently has a workman available who is able to do the unskilled tasks such as polishing and stripping at fairly low cost. If the dealer sends a piece of furniture out to an independent restorer he will probably pay less than a private person for the work he wants done. The dealer may be a competent restorer himself, and indeed it is interesting that a good number of the old established dealers who are members of the British Antique Dealers' Association are capable of good restoration work and have workshops well equipped for the purpose. A large dealer will have perhaps three restorers at work and it is not unknown for some dealers to have as many as a dozen or more at work on restoration.

A dealer will need to make a profit on the restoration work he has done himself, or had done by his men or his independent contractor, but the extent of that profit is, of course, a matter for him. It appears that some do not put as high a mark-up on restoration work as they do on the cost price of their furniture.

HOME RESTORATION

While in no way wishing to dash enterprise and enthusiasm, it is most important to realise the risks attendant upon home restoration. **If in doubt, leave well alone** should be the golden rule. This may sound extreme, but the salerooms are often lined with the incompetent attempts at restoration by amateurs who were ignorant of the essentials and ventured beyond their capabilities.

The most cogent deterrent for the incompetent or unknowledgeable restorer is the fact that rather than increasing the value of furniture, he can easily diminish it. Further expense may be necessary to undo the damage before more effective restoration may commence. For example, a major saleroom recently put up for auction a red walnut wine table, of the period of George II (about 1740) and one of the most desirable pieces of small antique furniture. The previous owner had detected some instability of the top of the table and inserted a very large steel screw through the top to fix it securely to the stem of the column, splitting the stem in the process. Extensive repairs were required and carried out, and the table fetched a smaller sum of money and will in the future never be as desirable as had the amateur never set hands on it.

You may say that this is all very well with fine furniture but what about cheap furniture on sale for a few tens of pounds? The answer is that yes, there is much more sense in embarking personally on restoring furniture which has little or no value, but what is inexpensive today may be very expensive tomorrow. For example, the Scottish designer Charles Rennie Mackintosh made a writing desk which was sold in the thirties for £25 but which made £80,000 in 1979. Lesser cases are likely to be quite common. Remember, **if in doubt, leave well alone.**

Upholstery

Although it is possible to study the craft of upholstery from a book it is by no means the best way for everyone. Some people have a natural aptitude for handicrafts; they require little instruction and supervision. For them the difficult skills which take most of us many hours of diligent practice to acquire are neither skilled nor difficult. For such people it is an extravagance to hand over furniture to a professional upholsterer if they have the time to do it themselves. They can easily learn from a book, but for the average person the most usual course is to apply to your local education authority for details of evening classes. Make sure that the course includes some instruction for those who wish to upholster antique furniture. What normally happens is that.the course starts on how to upholster drop-in seats to dining chairs then goes on to the more complicated tasks. Not always taught, but well worth understanding, is the art of making loose covers. They are the most useful and economical way of dealing with fairly modern furniture which is covered adequately (that is the fabric is sound) but in a colour or pattern which is unsuitable. They also protect better material and it was for this purpose that they were originally used.

What many upholsterers fail to tell their pupils is that techniques of upholstery change from one period in history to another. There is a tendency at the moment to overstuff upholstery, appropriate for nineteenth but not always for eighteenth-century furniture. Consult an expert before embarking on something dating, say, from before 1830. And in most cases it is safer to leave experts to do the work on the better specimens rather than making an attempt yourself.

Despite the great popularity of synthetic velvets and 'antique' hide it should be emphasised that there are alternatives, very commonly more appropriate and perfectly capable of fitting into modern interior schemes. Those who feel more ambitious can search antique shops for antique textiles with which to cover furniture – quite a number of shops keep stocks, often cheaper than modern equivalents, and salerooms also have textile sales. It is possible even to buy lengths of antique silk suitable for upholstery for as little as about five pounds per metre. But do not use a material which is likely to rot too soon – a dress fabric has a very short life if used to cover a chair. Good period inspired fabrics are widely available in most department stores or fabric shops so the upholsterer is not restricted to plain colours. It is fairly uncommon for upholstery significantly to diminish the value of any piece of furniture, although the buyer of a hideously upholstered piece would expect a price low enough to enable him to embark on reupholstery.

In some cases you may wish to keep the original material on the chair but the stuffing or springs have gone so it has to be removed. This gives you the opportunity of cleaning the fabric. Sometimes this proves to be impracticable, but the textile can still be reused, even if it has to be restored or fixed to a new cover by appliqué.

'Touching up'

This is a great temptation for any buyer and will apply to the buyers of furniture in the lower price range more than any other. The classic example is the gilt mirror found in a street market for under ten pounds. It is a plaster mirror and damp or knocks have caused a good deal of flaking off of the gold leaf so that it presents a fairly sorrowful appearance. It is not worth having gold leaf applied professionally; this, as already mentioned, is a very expensive task.

So what should the owner do? It is probably too difficult for a private person to water-gild the mirror with the help of information gleaned from do-it-yourself books. The cost of a single book of leaf gold is about ten pounds. Burnishing might well destroy the weakened plaster anyway. It is quite a good idea to watercolour the white plaster with an ochre tone, often in fact the tone of the bole, or fine clay, which is part of the undercoat for the gold leaf. The effect is by no means too bright and often looks very satisfactory.

Alternatively a gold oil paint might be applied; this is extensively available from art shops. This latter course is rather more problematical as you will end up with two tones of gold on the frame of the mirror, highlighting the repairs in most cases. So this should only be embarked upon when the damage is slight. Do not use this material (which comes in liquid or paste form) to repaint a frame completely; the effect is cheap and nasty. I have, however, seen some very ornate late Victorian plaster frames done in this way when the alternative was throwing them out altogether and must conclude that the effect was not absolutely disastrous.

But this is just one form of 'touching up'. The essence of the art is seeking to cover up something small either by a correct technique of restoration or by a makeshift way which serves as a deception to the casual eye. There can be no objection to the first course and for the cheaper type of purchase there seems to be little objection to the latter so long as no material destruction comes about. A missing chunk of wood from a drawer can be filled in with plastic wood, or simply painted to simulate the surrounding wood in the manner of *trompe l'oeil* art. Although the owner can nearly always spot this type of restoration, it is quite remarkable how few of your friends will ever notice such work provided it is carefully done.

Cleaning as restoration

Put bluntly, cleaning is the most useful restoration work the ordinary householder can do. Accretions of dirt which in no way enhance the furniture can be removed. There is a slight difficulty, however, in that some dirt can enhance furniture. A walnut bureau which has been wax polished since it was made, say, in the early eighteenth century will have developed a waxed skin we call a patina which adds materially to the value of the piece. It is by no means easy to fake, and mere approximations are arduously produced over a good period of time. In this skin is dirt, and in the crevices and scratches on the surface is yet more dirt which articulates and deepens the colour. What is important in the process of cleaning is that this valuable skin should never be destroyed.

It will often happen that such a walnut bureau will come into the owner's possession in need of a clean: it might have been waiting in a store for several months. The surface should be wiped over with a scarcely moist cloth dampened with a dilute mixture of vinegar to remove surface dirt and greasy substances and then dried *immediately*. The same process should be applied to every surface of the interior, removing all drawers and cleaning inside the carcass. Then the brasswork should be cleaned with a good proprietary brass cleaner and finally the surface should be polished with a good quality wax polish (silicone free). This is all preventative work for it helps to stave off inside woodworm.

Paintwork can be cleaned when badly grimed but care should also be taken to use a dirt solvent which does no damage. The best way to test it is to try out the cleaning in a small and inconspicuous corner, preferably not at all visible. The extent to which all the dirt should be removed is a matter of taste, but too vigorous a clean can deprive painted furniture of much character and give it an undue emphasis which is as unexpected as it is unappealing.

Metalwork should be removed when possible if it is in a bad state of corrosion. After treatment it should be carefully replaced and with luck should fit back with no sign of having been removed. Ironwork can seldom be removed from oak furniture and rust has to be carefully cleaned in position. Both brass and iron and, less commonly found on English furniture, ormolu or gilt metals, have a patina of their own which should be carefully preserved. Iron in particular is often polished up to a shiny white metal. This is not restoration and destroys the character of the metal. Never use a sand-blaster on iron.

Gilded furniture has to be cleaned with the greatest care as the gilding is on a plaster base which often expands on dampening and flakes off the gilding. Oil-gilded furniture which does not have a plaster base can be very gently dabbed with a damp chamois cloth. Dusting lightly is the best method, but a very careful scraping at thick dirt can flake away the dirt and leave the gold leaf intact. Attempt this with scrupulous care and stop immediately the process is seen to be ineffective. Traditionally a thin coat of size was always applied to protect the gold leaf.

Better left undone

(i) Do not attempt to tighten up chairs which have weak joints unless you have been trained to do this type of work. The success of strong glues to hold joints together is invariably short-lived and the subsequent repairs needed can be much more complicated as a result of this initial interference.

(ii) Do not attempt to replace legs in similar circumstances except where the value of the chair is slight. Chair legs have to be very strong and indifferent repairs have an unfortunate habit of letting down the owner or his guests with doubly damaging consequences.

(iii) Do not try and carve wood if you have no experience; you are likely to be in need of restoration yourself if you do.

(iv) Leave the skilled tasks of full-scale gilding and veneering to the experts.

(v) Never attempt anything you can't finish.

WHICH RESTORER TO CHOOSE

What should you do when you have a piece of furniture which needs restoration and needs a skilled hand to do it? Although most collectors will know of a good number of dealers they will perhaps know no restorers, whether as a branch of an antique dealer's trade or an independent individual. There are plenty of restorers to whom you can apply for most types of restoration, but the volume of work they are handling is so great that although they may take on your restoration it is with no promise as to when it will be done. The position is more acute with the best type of restorer who is continually in demand, mainly by dealers. In the case of a distinguished restorer of gilding, leading dealers are prepared to leave mirrors worth perhaps £10,000 or more in his hands for as long as a year. One does not need to be a financial wizard to understand how the interest on capital tied up for so long is paid for.

There are all types and conditions of restorer. At the top are men of the greatest skill and distinction; below them people who produce good quality restoration which would satisfy the high requirements of dealers in the British Antique Dealers' Association; below this grade are other restorers of varying qualities – some specialist, some general. It is not difficult as a rule to discover who is in the top two categories; they have a good reputation and are easily approached. But the third group is difficult to assess and the following section suggests some methods of sorting out the sheep from the goats. On balance private owners of antique furniture do not make enough enquiries as to who is a suitable restorer, assuming they are all equally capable. This is not true of the top restorers let alone of the lesser ones.

First of all ask the most reputable dealer you know who would be the best restorer to go to, specifying the type of restoration required. Sometimes a dealer is very much disinclined to help, preferring to keep the name of some particularly good restorer to himself, but on balance they are helpful and are pleased to make some recommendation. If you have a good piece of furniture it is often worth asking the furniture department of your local museum for the names of any good restorers in the region. The British Antique Dealers' Association and also the London and Provincial Antique Dealers' Association are often prepared to forward the appropriate information.

The British Art & Antiques Yearbook (updated annually) contains a list of trade services and suppliers which includes a fairly long list of the main restorers throughout the country, most of whom are thoroughly reputable. Other trade directories are helpful. Some members of the Guild of Master Craftsmen restore furniture. Their address is 10 Dover Street, London W1 (01-493 7571) and it is useful to apply to them for a list of craftsmen who are, as one might expect, highly competent in this technical field. The other immediate source is the 'Antique furniture restorers' Section in the Yellow Pages of your local telephone directory. But such a list would need to be vetted by reference to good reputation or by personal inspection.

Having come across a restorer one should make local enquiries of dealers as to his reputation. But the best test is to go straight to him and ask to see some of his work. This can be done simply by calling on him in his workshop for usually there will be examples of finished work awaiting collection.

Ask for an estimate and also for a written guarantee. The importance of an estimate cannot be overstated; restoration is usually expensive, and usually more expensive than you think. As for the written guarantee, it is not always possible for a restorer to give one but it may well be that he is prepared to give some form of a guarantee for such work as rejointing chairs.

It is useful to go to the restorer with a good idea of the kind of work you require, for as has been stated in Chapter 3 there are degrees of restoration. If, on inspecting the other pieces in the restorer's workshop, you find the result somewhat glossy, it is not a tactless thing to indicate your personal preference for a less bright finish. But always listen to the opinions of the restorer who will usually have experience on his side. When the furniture has been restored it will seldom look exactly as you want it; this is also true in many cases of picture restoration. Do not be alarmed. The effect is best judged some time after the work has been completed, when the tone has softened and the polish had a chance to build up through domestic attention.

UNRESTORED OR RESTORED – WHICH TO BUY?

Unrestored

(i) An unrestored example should be considerably cheaper than one which is restored.

(ii) A buyer is not obliged to embark immediately on the costly course of restoration; delay is often wise because the style and extent of restoration is never a cut and dried affair.

(iii) The buyer has a say in what sort of restoration is carried out. Certain types of antique shop exhibit the variety of tastes in restored furniture. There are some dealers who sell highly restored pieces, polished up to a dazzling brilliance, with gilding highly burnished and leather table tops new and brightly gilded. On the other hand there is the dealer who does a minimum of restoration to a piece of furniture, being content with giving each piece a good waxing and replacing missing pieces of veneer. Such a dealer will not remove ink stains on bureaux because he believes this is taking restoration too far. This is the type of choice the buyer has to make, and a choice is surely preferable to having a piece of furniture well but essentially arbitrarily restored.
(iv) You can wait many months for some restorations.

Restored
(i) Above all, there is no time wasted while waiting for restorers.
(ii) The buyer normally has no responsibility in making an error of judgement in respect of ordinary restoration which later turns out to be unacceptable when the question of resale emerges. He can return the goods if they turn out to be unsatisfactory.
(iii) Restored furniture is usually not cheap. Frequently dealers do not bother to restore furniture unless they are satisfied that they can get a good price for it.
(iv) The buyer has to accept what he is offered.

LOOKING AFTER FURNITURE

A little care in looking after one's furniture is a useful investment and always to be recommended. It can prolong its life or enhance or at least maintain its value. When you see furniture lined up at auction sales, you cannot help but note the decay which has been allowed to invade many lovely or practical pieces. In many cases much of this decay could have been arrested by simple maintenance in keeping with domestic uses. The result is that the vendor does not do as well as he might, and some buyers are dissuaded from making any bid at all for fear that restoration might be expensive.

There are five main steps that can be taken towards looking after your furniture.

(1) Furniture must be kept clean as superficial dirt, especially grime, is frequently destructive as well as being unattractive to the eye. Whereas those who live in the country are less affected by this problem, town dwellers are vulnerable. Upholstery is the worst affected and a vacuum cleaner can frequently be used to good effect.

(2) When you first acquire a piece of furniture it may prove vulnerable to shrinkage in its new environment, particularly if there is central heating. As soon as you acquire the piece give it a good dressing with linseed oil on all surfaces except the insides of drawers. This will help prevent the wood drying out, with the consequent splitting of veneers. It can with advantage be repeated every six months in an average centrally-heated house.

(3) Polish also has the effect of keeping the wood in good heart, as well as improving its appearance. Once a good depth of polish has been built up (see page 36) furniture should require no more than a light application every fortnight or three weeks. Good proprietary brands of wax polish are commercially available in hardware stores and in many antique shops. Some dealers make their own polish and retail it. Both hard wax and soft wax varieties are available, but what you should not use is a polish which contains silicone as it is thought not to be beneficial to antique furniture. For old oak,

dark wax varieties are available; for light woods like pine and satinwood use clean white wax polish. Those who feel adventurous can make their own beeswax polish in accordance with recipes used by Chippendale and Sheraton. Very good they are too, though very dangerous to make (the beeswax is diluted by the addition of heated methylated spirits – no naked flames!). But providing a good commercial brand is used this recipe is in no way superior.

(4) To prevent wood drying out badly it is well worth investing in a humidifier which will keep the atmosphere in a centrally-heated house sufficiently humid to preserve the furniture from damage. Electric versions are available for a little over £20, well worth the investment, or inoffensive troughs to hang on radiators can be purchased for about £5. A concealed bucket of water is a perfectly adequate makeshift.

(5) Finally, it is important to use furniture with regard to its condition. For example a veneered chest of drawers with veneered bracket feet should never be dragged across the floor as it is almost certain that pieces of veneer will eventually come loose. Similarly, frail bamboo bedroom chairs should not be treated as everyday dining chairs by a family of heavyweights. Again, this is essentially a matter of common sense.

WOODWORM

Woodworm is invariably caused by the furniture beetle and the tell-tale holes these pests leave used to be a sentence of death on furniture. The beetle may be dead and the holes merely memorials, but if powdery wood falls out when the hole is tapped this is not usually the case. It is rash ever to assume that the worm is completely dead and the best counsel is to buy a small bottle of a proprietary brand of killer with a small nozzle designed for penetrating wood holes and to use it on the diseased wood.

In pine the worming has often gone so far that a thorough repair is required, such as replacing a leg on a table which might otherwise collapse. Stripped pine which has been dipped in caustic soda usually has the worm destroyed. As pine is the most vulnerable wood it should be wiped with a good wood preservative.

If possible, examine the interior carcass of veneered furniture, particularly the feet which are especially vulnerable. The worm often consumes the carcass leaving the surface, especially if mahogany or rosewood, quite untouched. Precautionary treatment is desirable: use a preservative and give furniture a good brush in nooks and crannies.

5
Furnishing a House or Flat

IT is one of the oldest misconceptions in the history of interior decoration as practised by the amateur that it is impossible to mix old furniture with new. First of all, this was never historically true. In the early ages of furniture we find that styles were readily intermixed and furniture was handed down from one generation to another. With the passage of time furniture became more common and newer styles were introduced which fitted in with and were used with furniture of earlier periods. Paintings survive which show that old furniture and new were used together.

It was in the eighteenth century that the idea of rapidly changing fashion took hold. A cabinet maker would show himself only too able to keep abreast of the times and the published illustrations of Thomas Chippendale, for example, show a readiness to keep up to date. But at the same time Chippendale was making case furniture which was in few respects dissimilar from furniture which had been made twenty years earlier. It seems most likely that only in major interior redesigning was out-of-date furniture actually discarded. Records show that the cost of such schemes prevented regular redesigning of the kind that characterises a fashionable household in New York or San Francisco today. Photographs of nineteenth-century interiors show that a wide variety of styles were used together, and these photographs are not just records of the interiors of antique collectors but of a good cross-section of typical rooms.

It seems clear, therefore, that old and new, one style and another, have always been mixed. There are indeed various types of room, designed by one man at one time, which are as successful when recreated today as when they were conceived, despite subsequent changes in taste. But few of us are sufficiently wealthy or rarefied in our ambition to do other than adapt the examples of the past to contemporary needs. Most of us wish to live comfortably, surrounded by attractive and functional things; here something modern, here something old, here something pretty, here something of sentimental value and there, in the corner, the television set.

An excellent example of modern furniture commonly used with antiques is the upholstered suite of lounge chairs, usually two armchairs and a large sofa. Although not all styles are wholly successful with antiques, the regularly shaped sofas made by fashionable companies are outstandingly successful and are probably more commonly used with antique furniture than antique sofas themselves. Even the most *avant garde* furniture is equally capable of being used in conjunction with antiques, although this is clearly going to be much more controversial. The television set is perhaps the most prominent piece of furniture to figure in many rooms, even those with many antiques on display. Although there are cabinets made in the manner of period furniture, these are thoroughly unconvincing and generally of very poor quality. It seems better to make use of up-to-date styles of television set, not masquerading as antique but absolutely of the 1980s.

ONE ANTIQUE IN A MODERN ROOM

Even if the buyer prefers to stick to modern furniture there is still a case for displaying one old piece of furniture – many people have one or two such pieces handed down. These are normally placed nervously out of sight in a narrow passage or a box room on the assumption that they do not 'go'. This view is nearly always wrong, for a piece of antique furniture can often act as a focal point or an interesting point of contrast which can give character to a room. Certain examples of furniture are specifically purchased with this aim in view. Apparently the Davenport desk, a small desk with drawers at the side and a sloping top (see page 80), is much purchased by people who have no other antique furniture but who admire the form. Victorian spoon-backed *papier mâché* chairs (see page 68) are collected almost as sculpture. On a grander scale one hears of film stars buying important pieces of Victorian furniture, notably that designed by William Burges, clearly not for their utility. Some of the finest specimens of the highest quality Art Deco furniture are displayed on a raised plinth as if they were Rodin bronzes.

So although it is difficult to argue that by utilising just one piece of antique furniture in the above way you are actually *furnishing* a home, you are, nevertheless, doing on a somewhat rarefied scale what the average collector is doing; deriving pleasure from the possession of antique furniture.

WHAT WON'T GO WITH WHAT

Inevitably you will find yourself with one antique which clashes with another. Do not strain to force the two together. In most cases it is possible but it requires a degree of ingenuity in interior design which is beyond the average householder. Yet there are popular notions that certain things will not fit together when in fact, despite preconceived ideas, they will.

Oak and mahogany can go together perfectly well if they are tonally allied. It is rare that they are so similar that dining chairs and tables can be combined, but very often a dark oak bureau will sit quite well in a room which is furnished predominantly with mahogany. A less extreme case is the assumption that oak and fruitwoods are unacceptable together, or fruitwoods and mahogany, and again these rules are best disregarded as a general principle.

Oak and rosewood, however, seldom match well. Care also has to be taken in combining a mixture of stylistically dissimilar furniture. A more pronounced style will always tend to dominate. Victorian and country furniture seldom fit easily into the same room and Gothic and Chinese styles are not too easily brought together. Gothic and simple Regency, on the other hand, can be juxtaposed with reasonable success.

All this can make 'open plan' life rather difficult and there is much to be said for the use of a screen to break up a clear line of decorative disagreement. But as long as specific groupings are made which distinguish one style from another the problems should be lessened. The main thing to remember is that there are no hard and fast rules as regards what goes with what. The jacket photograph, for example, shows a thoroughly successful room, containing furniture of various periods and made of pine, fruitwood, beech, yew, rosewood, cane and walnut (box on coffee table).

THREE MAJOR CONCERNS

The collector of limited means will always be looking for areas where bargains may still be had. Furniture which has changed its function is an obvious choice (see page 9). In other cases furniture has been physically altered to turn it into an object suitable for use in an antique setting. The classic example is a Georgian square piano, many of which have been ruthlessly converted to sideboards. Similarly a small commode might have been converted into a drinks cabinet, or a pole screen used to form the base of a wine table. But in addition to being economical the average householder will want his furniture to be comfortable, practical and suitably informal.

Comfort

For most people this requirement is paramount, but frequently they do not realise that comfortable does not always look comfortable. A Louis XV armchair, which by common accord is one of the most comfortable chairs ever made, is often disregarded by those who feel that this cannot possibly be true of anything with wooden, slightly padded arms. It is related, however, that French princesses of the time declined to go into nunneries on the grounds of being unable to renounce the secular armchair.

Always test a piece of furniture for comfort bearing in mind every single use to which you intend to put it. Dining chairs may be required for other purposes, perhaps for sitting to write at a bureau or for bringing into use occasionally when the neighbours drop in. Even for normal use, if the joints have gone the diner will be in discomfort for fear of being let down ignominiously. Tables with a low rail can be agony for the tall.

A comfortable armchair may need to be reupholstered and this may cause a complete change in the feel of the chair. In time sheer use will make it more (or perhaps less) comfortable. Chairs take on the shape of their owners and this perhaps goes some way to explaining why old people prefer to leave their hideously unsprung furniture unrepaired. The other thing that ought to be said is that if you have a chair which is fairly uncomfortable but which has good period upholstery in good condition, do think very hard before you make any changes: you may easily diminish its value.

Practicality

'Practical' is a difficult word to define, but in essence it implies utility in respect of function. Antique furniture does not always have this quality, but in many cases its manufacture has been part of a continuing development in which style and fashion have been moulded by practical considerations through trial and error. Practicality is most often called into question in the case of kitchen furniture – 'Is it easy to clean?'; 'Won't pastry get squashed into the dropleaf of the table?' – these are the sort of questions people ask. Often a preference for things old will override a sense of the purely practical.

Bedroom furniture is another area where antique pieces may be more practical than it may seem. In terms of cost, it may be expensive to have a new mattress made for an old bed, but the price will probably compare favourably with the outlay on a modern bed. A large wardrobe may appear impractical until the space inside, subdivided into hanging areas and shelves, has been compared with the modern alternative of the fitted cupboard. Antique furniture is impractical only where it has been purchased with insufficient thought as to the function it is expected to perform.

Informality

The purchase of an antique chair does not condemn its owner to a lifetime of unremitting formality. Very few pieces of antique furniture available on the market were intended to be used in any more formal scheme of design than we are used to today. Students of Georgian interiors will notice that furniture was grouped against the walls when not in use, but when it was being used was probably positioned in a much more haphazard way than would be normal in the twentieth-century room. In the seventeenth century furniture would have been grouped round the fire in the same convivial manner of today.

This informality makes a striking contrast with interior designs using modern furniture, illustrated frequently in glossy magazines. There is usually a clear formality of design which is, of course, frequently dictated by the limited space available. A room furnished with antiques is likely to be more flexible and less formal than a modern scheme, and this informality is thoroughly in keeping with the way in which the furniture was originally used. The ultimate in informality is the cottage interior, combining Victorian and some country pieces with no special overall decorative scheme in mind save to amalgamate as much as possible and as decoratively as possible. Untidy people should always aim for an informal scheme, saving themselves from a life either of guilt or of continual tidying up.

THE SMALL FLAT

It is silly to pretend that today's buyers of antique furniture live in old rectories, manor houses or castles. The reality is more likely to be a tiny flat (indeed some well known collectors are forced by the cost of their collections to live in what amounts to no more than a bed-sitter). It is wrong to assume that antiques are always too large for modern living; many small examples are available, or one large piece can often look very effective in a small space.

Small tables that may have started life, for example, as Pembroke or Sutherland tables (see pages 60 and 59) are ideal for use as dining tables. Chairs originally intended for a bedroom are often on a smaller scale than dining chairs and although frail can be invaluable for occasional use. Corner furniture makes use of space that might otherwise be wasted. A converted commode makes a small chest of drawers. Throughout history small, sometimes tiny, pieces of furniture have been made, usually with ladies in mind. For example, something described as a lady's writing table is fairly certain to be petite, and a combination of delicate cabinet making and especially convenient size makes such pieces of furniture fairly expensive. A bachelor's chest, the only small masculine piece of furniture, is certainly extremely expensive, and an early Davenport (see page 80) or a joint stool are equally sought after.

Hard and fast strictures are undesirable, but in general it can be said that an over emphasis on dark and heavy furniture in a restricted space can create an atmosphere of gloom in which many people would prefer not to live. By a careful use of colour schemes, however, even dark furniture can be brought to life. Complementary antique artefacts, good and bright, are cheaply acquired (see page 50 for advice). By tradition brass and copper go well with oak but other even brighter ideas are feasible with a little thought and a short search. Painted furniture can look very striking in a flat. If you do go for darker pieces, consider the lighting very carefully. Strong source light beamed against a reflecting surface is an excellent way of achieving a brighter effect. If at all possible try to prevent strong lights from damaging or fading furniture.

THREE IMPORTANT ROOMS

Furnishing a kitchen

It is possible to furnish a kitchen using only antique pieces – even old stone kitchen sinks and brass taps can be found – but this is probably taking things to extremes. It is likely that a modern cooker, refrigerator, washing machine and boiler will be fairly dominant features, but beyond this antiques can be introduced with good effect. Old shop fittings can be successful as cupboard space and marble-topped washstands are extremely useful as dressers and working surfaces, ideal for making pastry and confectionery. There is every reason to include a dresser, the one piece of furniture intended for the kitchen, although the finest oak versions are not wholly suited to the grease and dirt a kitchen will create. A large pine table can serve as a working surface and also as a dining table, especially as kitchens are often a focal point of the household.

Modern air-expelling machines make kitchens less greasy and smoke-laden than they used to be and proprietary cleaners are efficient and speedy. It is important, however, to exercise care when choosing kitchen furniture. Pine, fruitwoods and oak are suitable but when veneered woods are used any dampness from the bottom of china or glasses can ruin their appearance. Highly polished surfaces are also easily damaged. Although not altogether to be recommended, wooden furniture that is not particularly valuable can be sealed with a polyurethane varnish. A large sheet of glass cut to size helps protect pine surfaces from burns.

For decoration, ceramics and metalware are the best idea as they can be cleaned easily. When pictures and posters are used they should be well sealed in their frames to protect them against steam and insidious grease.

Furnishing a dining room

Although not the most conspicuous feature of a dining room the most essential requirement is something to sit on; the dining chair section in Part II outlines the variety usually available. Dining rooms can vary enormously in appearance, but the more formal the furniture the more expensive it is likely to be. Chippendale mahogany chairs or formal neo-classical Regency styles are beyond the pockets of most buyers. But simpler Georgian mahogany chairs, or rosewood versions, are not specially expensive, particularly when collected in groups of two or four, slowly building up a set. Victorian chairs are even less expensive.

It certainly seems to be the case that the chairs should be the first purchase if possible, for they set the style of the room. A Chippendale mahogany style, for example, would more or less commit the buyer to a fairly formal room, whereas a set of Victorian balloon backed chairs gives more leeway. The same can be said of country chairs.

The dining table should come next. While you are looking (and it may take some time to find a suitable table at a price you can afford) a good interim measure is an old trestle or a chipboard tabletop to put over the top of a smaller table. A covering with a good cloth is essential to conceal the makeshift nature of the table. Stability is obviously also of paramount importance. Sideboards or dressers are usually expensive but some varieties are still available at a reasonable price, and these are included in the survey in Part II.

Formal dining rooms of the eighteenth century tend to have light-coloured decorative schemes, and the traditional method of decorating the walls is with prints. The prints themselves can still be obtained for small sums, but they should be framed and mounted as well as you can afford. Try to avoid the frames described as 'Hogarth'; they are cheaply gilded and ordinary. Old frames of good quality are usually the best but they are difficult to find. Nineteenth-century examples are more readily available. The Victorians thought the colour red was appropriate on the walls of a dining room; also that it was medically advisable as it was a stimulant to the appetite and an aid to digestion. There may be no truth in this but it is certainly a striking method of decorating and looks well with thick gilt frames. The dark tones of the room can conceal minor defects in the frames which are apt to show up in a room with lighter decoration.

Lighting in a dining room should emphasise the table, so candlelight should always be considered. Candles are also desirable on the sideboard to illuminate the serving point. Otherwise, choose diffused lighting that does not obtrude.

Furnishing a drawing room or lounge

Few people today have the space for a formal drawing room and a great deal of expense is involved in trying to furnish such a room successfully. Historically it was the principal entertaining room and the decoration by tradition was the most lavish in the house (with the exception of the seventeenth-century bedroom). Today it is still an important room for entertaining, but most people call it the 'lounge' or 'sitting room' and comfort is as important as display.

Even the dedicated collector of antique furniture will often prefer not to use an antique sofa; even when they are comfortable they do not allow the user to sit in the lounging way many people do today. Manufacturers have made a considerable range of sofas and easy chairs, often sold in 'suites', which fit in well and give a satisfactory degree of low-level comfort. This new low level makes necessary a table at a sympathetic height – the ubiquitous coffee table. Antique examples of this type of furniture are extremely rare and are often above the price range of the average buyer.

Easy chairs and low tables excepted, a great variety of antique furniture is available. Examples are illustrated in Part II, and the 'Miscellaneous' section in particular might yield some ideas. Two items which have not yet been considered are important in the decoration of a drawing room; they are the chimney piece and the fireside rug. The chimney piece has usually been removed from period houses and frequently does not exist at all in modern ones. Such is the native British feeling for a fireplace as the focal point of a home that one is often installed. Reproductions are available but it is frequently not realised that genuine examples can be had which are highly attractive and often cheaper than the reproductions. (If you buy marble do check to ensure that it is properly anchored to the wall and on a secure base.)

A hearthrug, it follows, is also important, and particularly conspicuous because of the low level of the seating arrangements. If a real fire is kept in then care must be taken to protect the rug with a guard against flying sparks. There are many specialist carpet dealers and it is best to go to one with a high reputation. The world of carpets is, in my view, much more complicated than that of antique furniture, and infinitely more controversial. In effect, if you are looking for an 'antique' or 'old' carpet (the terminology differs from furniture) you should go for a good quality functional carpet that is vegetable-dyed. For advice on buying a cheaper carpet, see page 51.

INEXPENSIVE DECORATIVE ANTIQUES WITH WHICH TO SET OFF YOUR ANTIQUE FURNITURE

Pleasing as antique furniture looks on its own, it is improved by the use of pictures and oddments of glass and china. These lend distinction and personality to any scheme. A number of the best known interior designers, before they start on a scheme for a client, set aside some of his effects and most treasured possessions to use to personalise the room when it is completed. This section concentrates on absolute economy while at the same time looking for good quality antiques. Nothing likely to cost over £50 has been included. Because the examples selected are for decorative purposes, and are not intended to be functional or bought purely as investment, some slight damage may be tolerated.

Pictures

It is often a bad economy to buy pictures which are already framed. The frame will represent a large part of the price and very often the collector can find a serviceable frame in a junk shop for a small sum. Also, by going to bookshops and to picture dealers you will usually find an album of unframed and unmounted pictures which need cost only a few pence. **It is still true today that, with luck, high quality English watercolours can be purchased for less than £10.** Although less common, attractive oil paintings, mainly of the nineteenth century, can be acquired from junk shops for a few tens of pounds. One of the most scholarly of London print sellers has a series of folios containing a constantly replenished stock of fine prints for less than ten pounds. As an example, a large, mid-eighteenth-century print of an elegant Roman vase by the famous artist, Piranesi, was selling in that shop for about that figure.

Old photographs, posters and handbills and general ephemera survive in very great numbers for little expense. Many frames are also available very cheaply so it is remarkable that there is any market at all for reproduction prints. They can cost much more than a good period print, which if carefully bought is likely to be a considerable investment in the long term. If an accurate period flavour is aimed for, that is where it is intended that prints should match the period of the furniture, then this can be achieved with no difficulty and without breaking your financial limits. Period frames are less easy to find, especially if the period predates 1800. With luck these do occasionally appear, but failing that some nineteenth-century frames, which are not expensive, can be made to serve in place of the earlier examples.

Ceramics and glass

In general, oak and country furniture is well set off by pottery whereas mahogany and rosewood show up well when used with porcelain. Walnut, on the other hand, is excellently set off by both. But these are only general rules.

Cracked vases and jugs, which are usually quite large, can with very little difficulty be converted into lamp bases. Damaged mid-nineteenth-century Delft, for instance, should not cost too much. It is not necessary to bore holes into the bases of the vases as modern electrical fittings can be inserted without going to these lengths. Plates and dishes to set off a Welsh dresser can be purchased inexpensively for a few pounds each. Porcelain, when damaged, is very good value for decorative purposes. In 1979 it was possible to buy for under fifty pounds red anchor Chelsea (c. 1753) in perfect condition; a good but damaged example cost fourteen pounds.

So both pottery and porcelain can be displayed either on a wall in conjunction with antique furniture or on the furniture itself; the collector has a great deal to explore. Particularly good value at the moment are nineteenth-century porcelain dinner plates, especially crested examples, and this is an excellent example of an inexpensive method of decoration.

A damaged glass decanter or a single glass candlestick can with little difficulty be converted into a lamp base. Perfect examples of old glass are now becoming somewhat expensive, so buy those specimens which have slight chips to their bases but which are still highly attractive; their defects are seldom noted. Victorian pressed glass still costs around ten pounds for quite good examples in perfect condition and other specimens of Victorian glass can be even better value. Edwardian cut glass is perhaps the most undervalued and a group of such glass can give a distinctive, somewhat feminine ambience to a decorative scheme. Any decorative plan which makes use of glass will require adequate lighting, without which any assembly of glass looks lifeless and dull.

Textiles

Textiles make a room more inviting. It is possible to buy curtains which are antique, or at least old, but textiles of considerable age tend to sell for fairly high prices. The salerooms in London sell much material to restorers for reupholstering furniture, which often explains the high price it fetches. Furthermore, old textiles are often very frail and are not necessarily the best way of setting off antique furniture. New material is available in styles which either imitate the styles of the past or are sympathetic with the styles of furniture with which they have to hang. A richer effect may be achieved by the use of trimmings and gimps which are now being made in greater numbers than before and showing considerable faithfulness to their eighteenth- and nineteenth-century progenitors.

Old cushions, modern cushions covered with lengths of old textiles, old embroidered runners and even old textiles used for lamp shades are all valuable ingredients in giving a room an interesting period flavour consistent with the use of antiques.

Finally, one of the more useful textiles is the carpet or rug, old examples of which are available in salerooms and in the shops of general antique dealers. Some rugs are fairly inexpensive, but they are not cheap when bought from specialist carpet dealers. Old Middle Eastern carpets which are well worn are excellent short term buys as they have a mellow appearance and an extraordinary resilience. Wear on carpets is usually quite visible, but it is sometimes possible to conceal a good deal of the worst patches by an ingenious arrangement of furniture.

PART TWO

Chairs

DINING chairs are surely one of the biggest expenses in building up a home. On the whole, examples have been grouped according to the price of a useful set. The problem with chairs is that prices do not increase in an ordinary arithmetical progression, that is, one chair costs ten pounds, two chairs cost twenty pounds, three chairs cost thirty pounds and so on. Sets of four, six and eight plus increase in price proportionately and the only way a collector will be able to buy six chairs for sixty pounds is by buying them one at a time.

A popular method is to collect a set of similar chairs, none of which is identical. In the case of simple country furniture this is a very acceptable course, as it is with Victorian balloon-backed chairs. In time you can trade in 'individuals' for more appropriate examples with certain helpful dealers.

There is no doubt that mahogany and walnut eighteenth-century sets are not going to cost less than £1,000, unless you are prepared to consider reproductions. There are nineteenth-century reproductions, such as those made by Edwards and Roberts, which are of very high quality and well worth considering. Later reproductions are expensive and not usually so well made. Some 'reproductions' are so misshapen as to be nightmarish.

Under £150	**£150–750**	**Over £750**
Country stick-back	Ladder-back	Hepplewhite
Thonet bentwood	Yorkshire	Queen Anne
Smoker's bow	Regency	Chippendale
Morris 'Sussex'	Windsor	
Utility		
Victorian stuffed-seat		
Windsor lath-back		
Balloon back		

This type of country stick-back chair is in elm, dating from about 1800. It has a saddle seat, which is more comfortable than it may appear. Examples which have lift-in upholstered seats are slightly more comfortable and more expensive; the use of yew and of fruitwoods such as apple and pear also makes them more expensive.
A *Single* **C** *Set of four*

Thonet bentwood chairs originated in Austria in the late nineteenth century but proliferated all over Europe, either made by Thonet or by rivals. They are made by using a steam process to bend wood. Dining chairs are not expensive and are often stamped or labelled *Thonet* inside the seat rails. A rocking version is illustrated on page 66.
A *Single* **B** *Set of six*

The smoker's bow is an excellent robust chair and is extremely comfortable. They are not usually found in sets, being most commonly intended for use in public houses and barbers' shops. Most examples are mid-nineteenth-century, made of elm, but fine mahogany Georgian examples can also be found.
A *19th century* **F** *Georgian Not made in sets*

The Morris and Company 'Sussex' chair was made from about 1865. This style which was outstandingly popular has a rush seat and was based on traditional country styles. Frequently they are found plain, or painted black with white painted banding. They are becoming expensive because of the Morris association.
A *Single* **C** *Set of four non elbow*

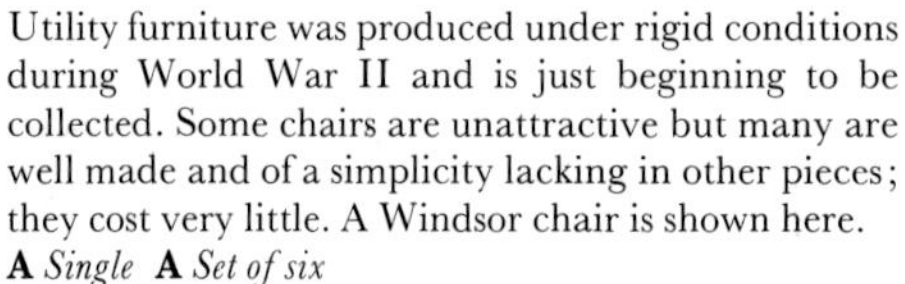
Utility furniture was produced under rigid conditions during World War II and is just beginning to be collected. Some chairs are unattractive but many are well made and of a simplicity lacking in other pieces; they cost very little. A Windsor chair is shown here.
A *Single* **A** *Set of six*

An upholstered Victorian chair in good condition is an excellent purchase. Many of these commercially produced chairs have elaborate interior springing.
A *Single* **C**+*Set of six*

The Windsor lath-back is a late type of Windsor chair, dating from about 1870 and later. Although it does not have the elegance of the more traditional pattern it is equally comfortable. A group of similar chairs fits well into a kitchen or country setting. Many examples still have their original painting; it is desirable not to remove any of this original surface.
A *Single elbow* **B** *Set of six non elbow*

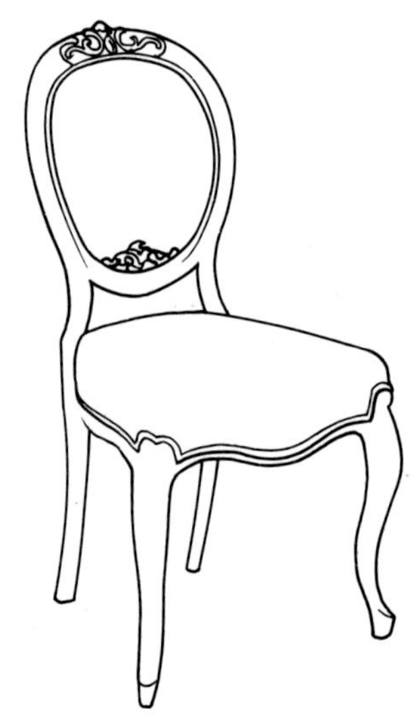

This is a typical mid-Victorian balloon-backed chair with a stuffed seat, though the form varied considerably throughout the period 1825–80 and even later. At one stage the balloon back was itself stuffed. Rosewood and walnut examples with cabriole legs are the best specimens, though mahogany is less expensive. Some bedroom specimens are of painted beech with caned seats, inexpensive but often too frail for using in a dining room.
A *Single* **C**+*Set of six*

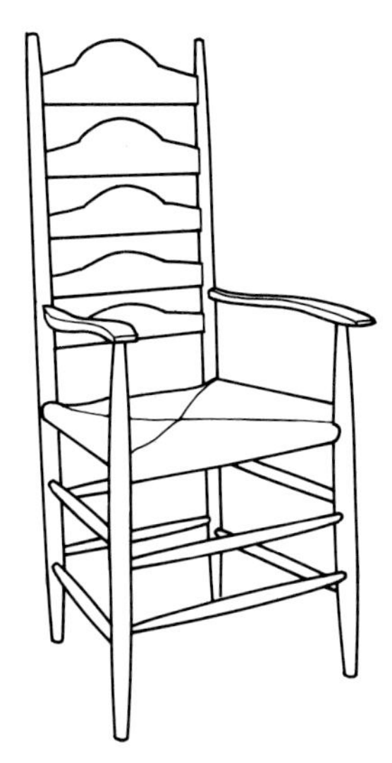

Ladder-back chairs are frequently encountered and you may expect to find eighteenth, nineteenth and twentieth-century examples. A good set from the eighteenth century may cost a lot of money but single examples and pairs need not be expensive. One of the keys to price other than date is patination. Illustrated here is a chair designed in the traditional idiom in the late nineteenth century by Ernest Gimson and put into commercial production.
A *Single 19th century* **F–H** *Set of six 19th century* **B** *Single 18th century* **J/K** *Set of six 18th century*

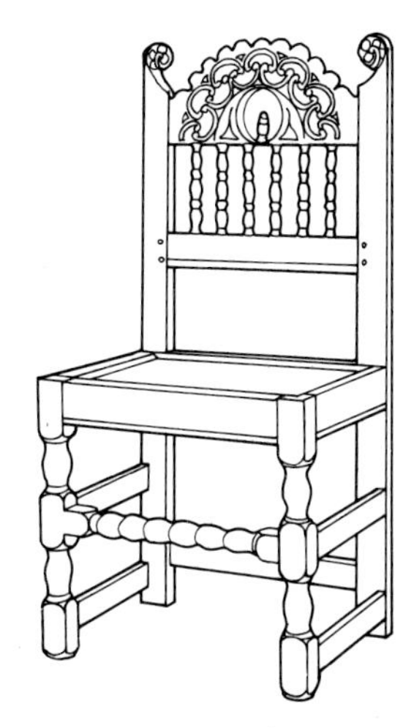

Provincial seventeenth-century chairs are rare and many have pronounced regional characteristics as in this Yorkshire chair of about 1680. Other chairs made about the same time are less expensive than those specifically associated with a more or less defined locality.
E–G *Single*

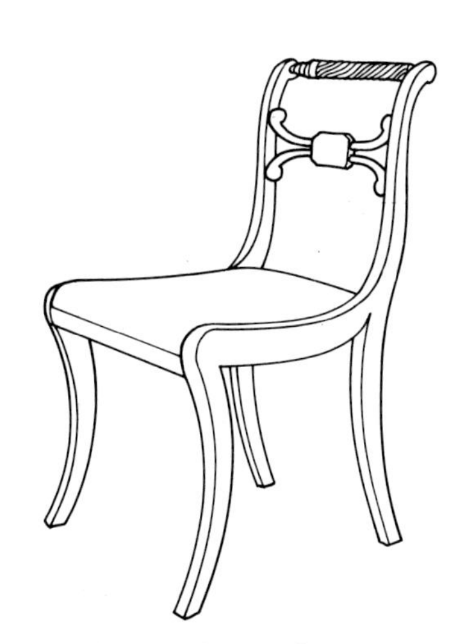

Regency chairs, usually in mahogany, rosewood or simulated rosewood have excellent classic features. Sabre legs and rope twist back splats (associated with the style of chair called a 'Trafalgar') are common.
B/C *Elbow* **B** *Non elbow* **H–K** *Set of six* **K** *Set of six with two elbow*

The classic Windsor chair was made from the early eighteenth century and throughout the nineteenth century. A Windsor chair is simply a chair in which the arms, legs and back splats are all fixed into the wooden seat. This version is early nineteenth century.
H *Single*

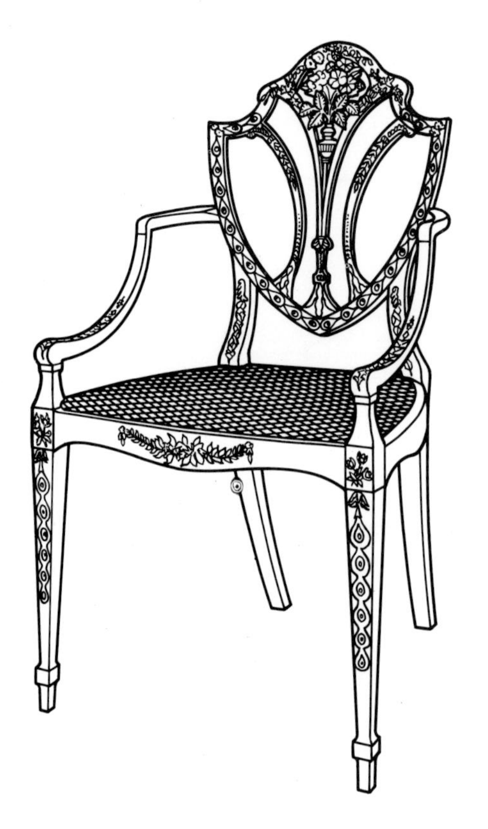

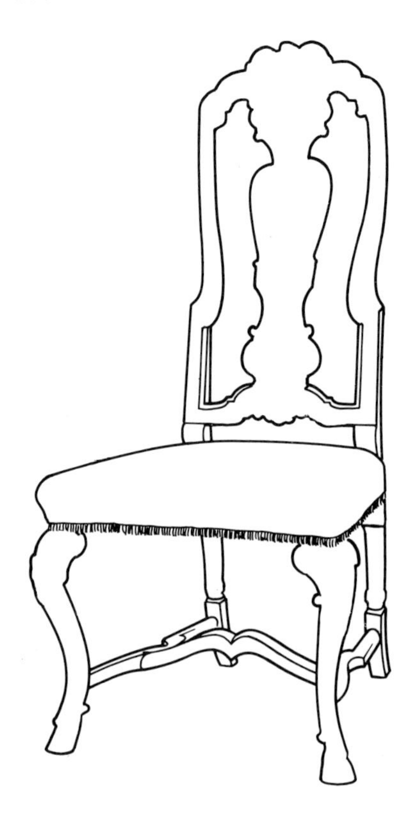

Above left: This type of eighteenth-century Hepplewhite shield back chair is highly desirable. The quality varies, but even the simplest are expensive.
D/E *Single* **K–M**+ *Set of six*

Above: Perhaps the rarest type of chair of good English make available is the 'Queen Anne' walnut variety. Walnut was used to best effect in the last decade of the seventeenth and first thirty years of the eighteenth centuries. Much walnut furniture has been faked and very little of good quality survives.
E+ *Single* **L** *Set of six*

Left: This type of chair is of the Chippendale period, dating from about 1765. Little furniture is directly attributable to Chippendale's workshops and even modest period examples are expensive.
D+ *Single* **K**+ *Set of six*

Dining Tables

HAVING purchased a set of dining room chairs, the other essential is something to eat off. Ideally the style of your chairs will dictate the style of table (or vice versa if the table has been acquired first). The aim of the buyer should be to find near contemporaries or, if country furniture, the same informal type. Prices depend very much on the number of people who have to be seated. Six to eight is usual for the average dining table. Eight- to ten-seaters are the most popular and measurably more expensive. It is uncommon, however, that many people sit down regularly in such numbers and a good solution is to buy a chipboard tabletop, hinged to hide away when not in use, and place it on top of a smaller table. Always protect the table with a baize cloth. But it is still possible to find large tables to seat upwards of eight in the lower price range, although these are usually unsuitable for more formal dining rooms.

Under £150	**£150–750**	**Over £750**
Art Deco	William IV library	Georgian pedestal
Oak gateleg	French provincial	George I walnut
Sutherland	Breakfast	
Pine kitchen	Mahogany oval dropleaf	
Oak dropleaf	Victorian expanding	
Pembroke		

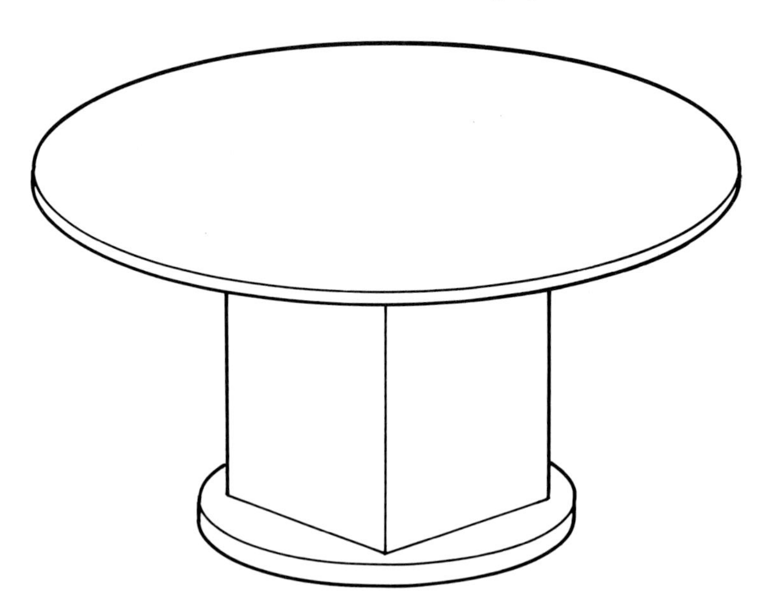

Art Deco styles are now fashionable and some small tables can be had for a modest outlay. In London the collector may have to search for some time but in the country surprising bargains can be had. The table illustrated is in black perspex and would just seat six.
C

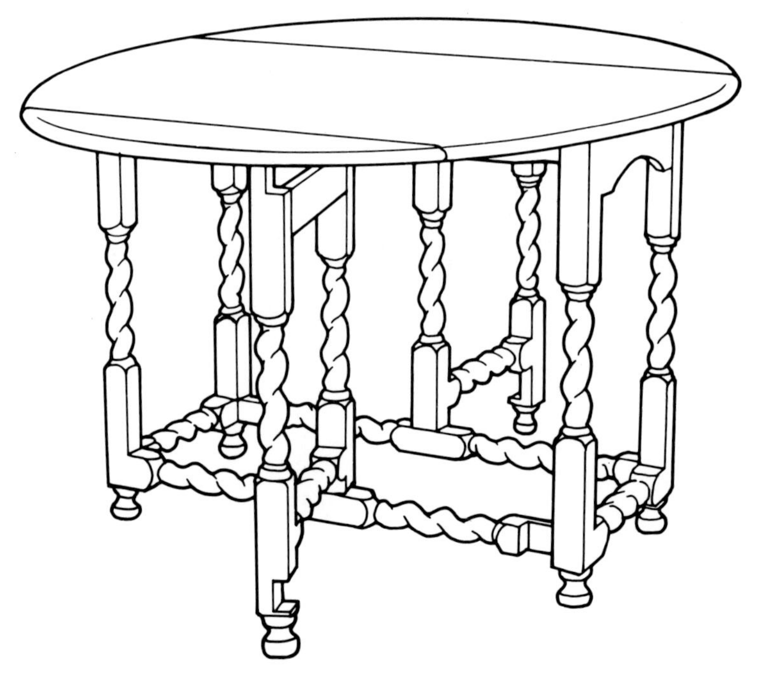

Oak gateleg tables with barley twist turned legs have been made since the middle of the seventeenth century. In this century they have been commercially produced on a large scale. They are, when the varnish is cleaned away, nice pieces of oak which after wax polishing will take on a genuine colour of their own. The type illustrated dates from the 1920s and will seat four to six.
B

Photo: courtesy of Christie's (South Kensington) Ltd

A Sutherland table is very similar to a Pembroke table, the main difference being that the centre portion is narrow, really no wider than a shelf. This example, dating from the 1880s, would seat up to six although in general they are not the most stable type of table. They are becoming expensive, but lesser examples can still be fairly cheap.
C+

Large, well worn, pine kitchen tables of the late nineteenth century are excellent value. They are even cheaper when the legs have not been stripped of their original paint and this can be removed with little difficulty. This table seats eight.
B+

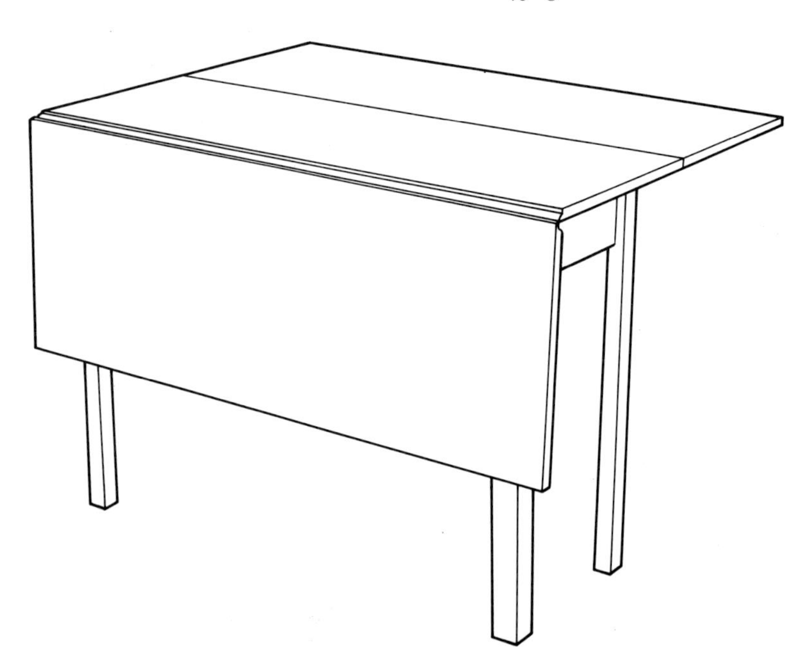

This type of early nineteenth-century oak gateleg table with wide fall flaps is large enough to seat eight. Tables like this are not rare and are found in mahogany as well as oak, though mahogany examples are approximately twice the price.
B+

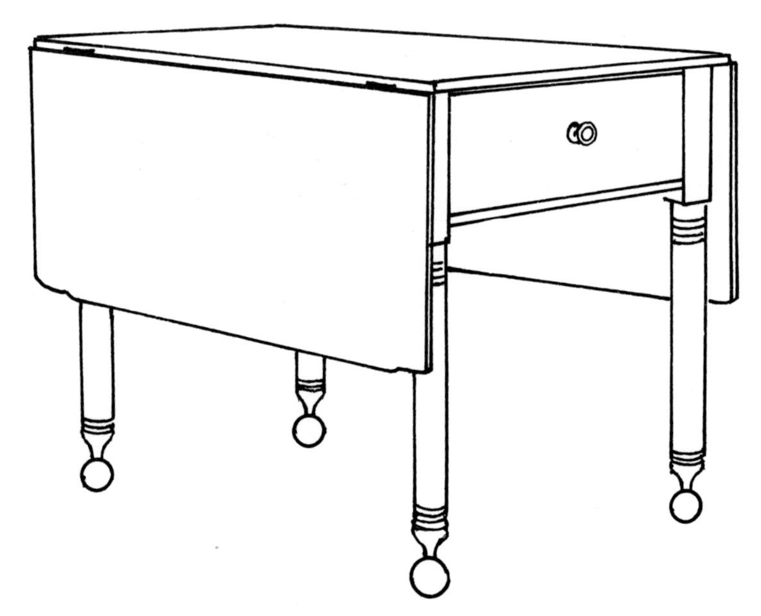

Pembroke tables vary in price. This is an American example of the nineteenth century, but English versions of the early years of the twentieth century are available with plain square and upturned legs. All are difficult to find in the lowest price category, but they do exist (I recently found two on the same day in a small Suffolk town). They can seat four to six.
C+

This William IV rosewood library table is large enough to seat six to eight people so is ideal as a dining table. These are not particularly common and examples are likely to be more simple than this fine specimen with its well carved legs.
H/J

Mid-nineteenth century French fruitwood tables are among the most easily obtainable of dining tables and appear to be imported into this country in considerable numbers. This example is in cherrywood.
G/H

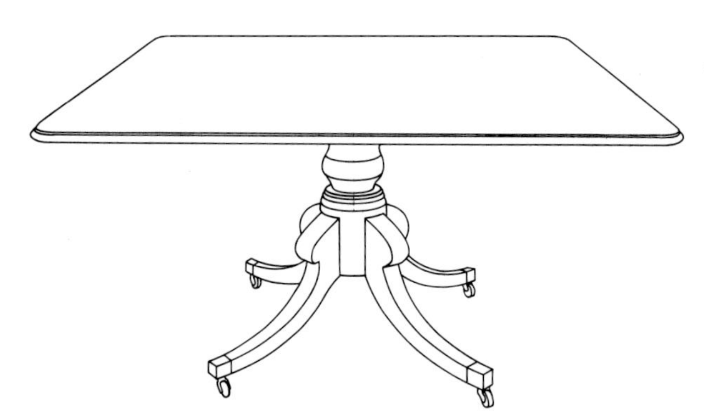

This type of Regency breakfast table dates from about 1810–15. They are usually in rosewood or mahogany, with restrained stringing and crossbanding and brass enrichments. About 153 cm (60 in) long and 102 cm (40 in) wide, it is the ideal table for a small flat and therefore expensive.
H+

This illustration shows a country oval dining table in mahogany (uncommon in such pieces) dating from about 1810. It is on the gateleg principle and this explains why it is fairly small; gatelegs become unstable when large.
F

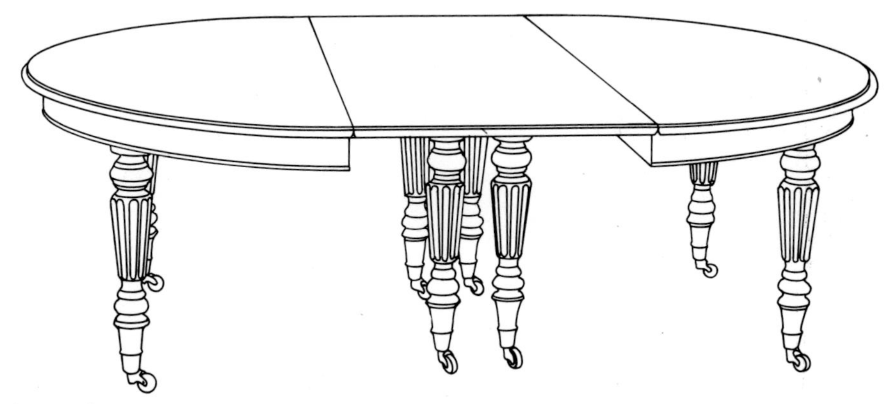

The large mahogany expanding dining table illustrated was made by Gillow and Company about 1880 and has the desirable feature of half oval ends. Price depends on the maximum extent, but only very large Victorian tables reach four figures.
H+

This example of a large-scale Georgian two-pedestal dining table dates from about 1790 and is in very good condition. Three and four-pedestal versions would be extremely expensive today.
L

This rare George I gateleg table is in red walnut and has a good colour and patina. The top is crossbanded and the square cabriole legs terminate in hoof feet.
M+

Easy Chairs

EASY chairs offer the prospective buyer a fairly wide choice, particularly in the lower price range. Comfort was not a conception that weighed heavily on people's minds in sixteenth and early seventeenth centuries. Cushions tended only to relieve discomfort. But the last twenty years of the seventeenth century saw efforts to increase comfort and the ever popular armchair was the great contribution; it is fair to say that the comfort of the wing chair has never been surpassed, even by the most sophisticated interior-sprung devices of the nineteenth and twentieth centuries. Interior springing made chairs comfortable without necessarily improving their looks.

Most upholstered pieces will have been reupholstered at some stage and it is important that sympathetic fabric should have been employed; synthetic velvet is not to be recommended though its use has become widespread. Some pieces retain their original upholstery and it is worth making the effort to preserve this: nobody should buy a wing chair with period tapestry if it is going to be subjected to unreasonable rough and tumble.

Some of the easy chairs included *look* uncomfortable, amongst them the Windsor armchair. I know of nobody who has said this type of chair *is* uncomfortable, and for the elderly and those who prefer a more upright posture they are second to none.

Finally, if you have chosen a modern 'suite' of furniture because of its special comfort, remember that this does not automatically confine you to the purchase of other pieces of modern furniture. Much antique furniture is complementary and certainly does not detract from modern pieces, a theme dealt with more thoroughly in Chapter 5.

Under £150	**£150–750**	**Over £750**
Commercial late 19th century	Corner chair	Queen Anne wing armchair
Morris 'adjustable'	Deep buttoned Victorian	Hepplewhite
Thonet rocking chair	Papier mâché	Fine French Louis XV
William IV library	Louis XV armchair	
'Comfy' Victorian	'Gothick' Windsor	

Commercially made in about 1875, this mahogany armchair is similar to pieces produced in America and Australia. It is very comfortable, with downswept arms and a rush seat, and is often used as a desk chair.
B

In the 1860s Morris and Company popularised this type of chair with an adjustable back. It was a style much in evidence abroad, even found in the Far East where its low slung form was widely popular, also being made in bamboo. They were not all as comfortable as Morris versions.
B

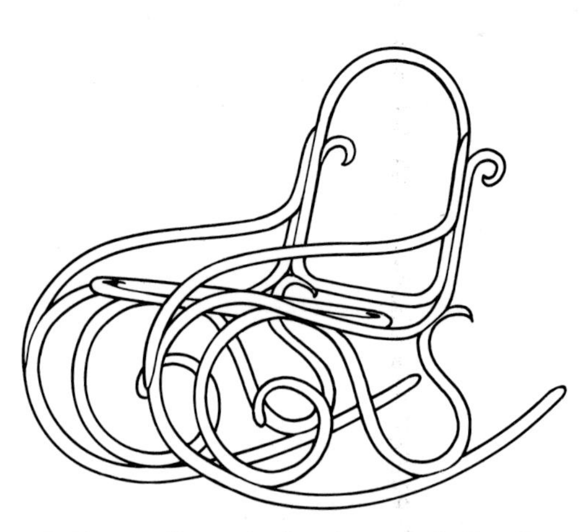

In Vienna, Thonet developed a method of bending wood by steam and his strong and inexpensive chairs were being manufactured by 1850. This example was made about 1875. They were widely exported, and later extensively copied: genuine pieces frequently have a label or a stamp on the frame. Variants are still being made to this day.
C

This type of large William IV mahogany library chair is usually undervalued. They are upholstered in red leather and the leather of the seat has frequently been renewed. This is a good comfortable, but masculine, chair. It is only just recognisable as being derived from Regency taste.
C

Late Victorian armchairs were made commercially in huge quantities and apart from being found in almost every home in the country were exported to America and the entire British Empire, particularly New Zealand and Australia. Today these can be bought cheaply at local auction sales and in junk and antique shops. They will usually need reupholstering, which will make them initially less comfortable than when 'tried out' in the shop.
A

This red walnut corner or writing chair has a drop-in seat. The pad foot is a good feature. Examples are found during the reigns of George I and II (1714–60) and they are extremely comfortable. Red walnut is characteristic of the period and is similar in colour to rich unfaded mahogany. Mahogany examples are also to be found.
F

The pair of Victorian 'Grandfather' and 'Grandmother' chairs below have been reupholstered, but in the correct style of deep buttoning. Needless to say, when sold separately the armchair commands a higher price. These are in mahogany, about 1870.
E

Right: Papier mâché is strong and perfectly usable. This spoon-backed armchair is black, with elaborate painted decoration and gilding, and inlaid with mother of pearl. It is stamped with the name of the principal manufacturer, Jennens and Bettridge, and dates from the 1840s.
H

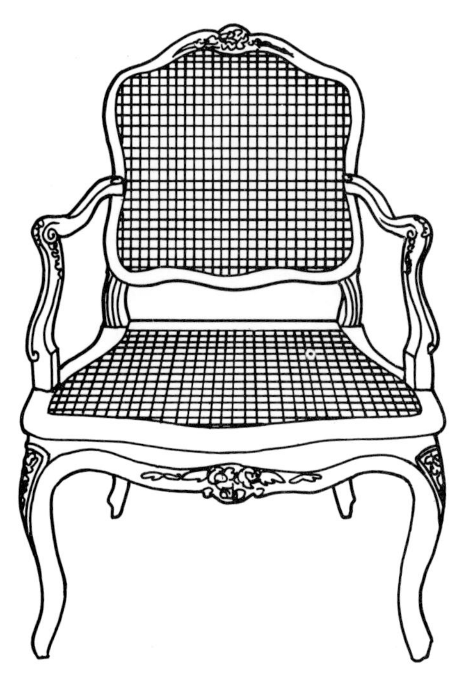

Above: A caned walnut Louis XV armchair, intended to take lavish stuffed cushions. It is a style of comfortable French chair that was imitated by Chippendale and his successors and occasionally they are found in this country, sometimes bearing the stamp of the maker. Versions are found of beech – sometimes gilded, sometimes painted – and wholly upholstered rather than caned. Restored they are very expensive but with luck good unrestored examples can be found.
E *Unrestored*

This is a good nineteenth-century Gothic chair. The range of Windsor chairs is so wide that it has resulted in a book devoted to them alone. The most difficult aspect is dating examples, but factors such as the wood they are made of (yew is desirable), any indication of origin and condition are responsible for the wide variation in price.
G (**D** *For more simple 19th century example*)

Right: Wing armchairs were made throughout the eighteenth century; the later in date the less expensive they become. The early ones are exceptionally expensive when in walnut, as are the versions made in the period of Chippendale. Original upholstery significantly increases the price. The Queen Anne example illustrated, of about 1710, has slightly unusual stretchers.
J–M

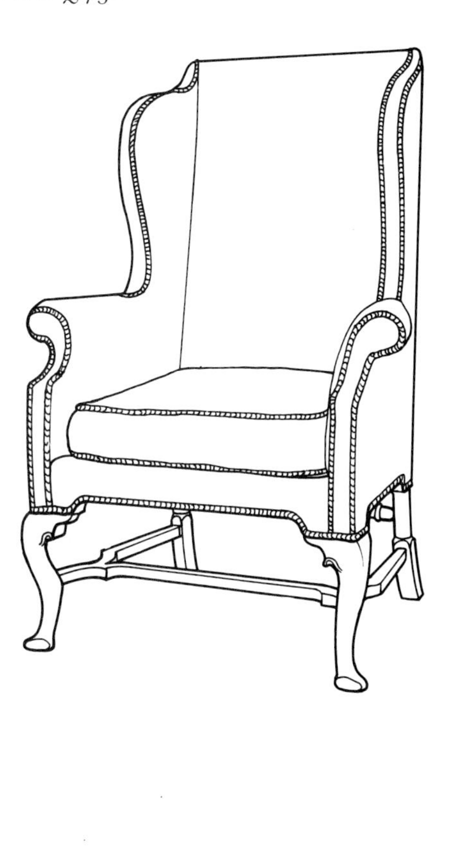

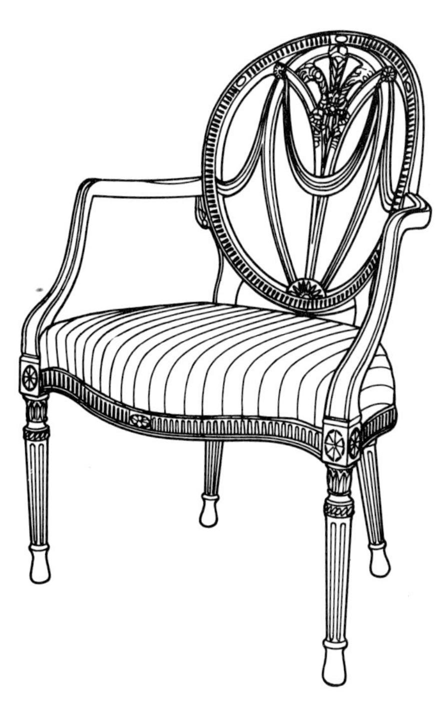

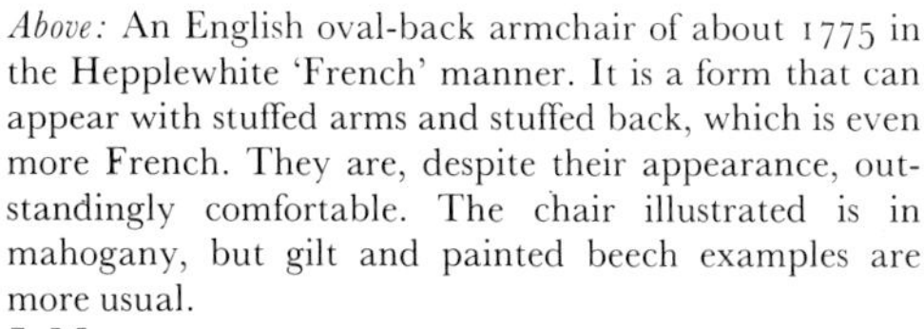

Above: An English oval-back armchair of about 1775 in the Hepplewhite 'French' manner. It is a form that can appear with stuffed arms and stuffed back, which is even more French. They are, despite their appearance, outstandingly comfortable. The chair illustrated is in mahogany, but gilt and painted beech examples are more usual.
J–M

This is a particularly fine French giltwood chair, usually upholstered in Beauvais tapestry, and is a good example of the best Louis XV style. Less good versions are as comfortable but not so well upholstered (original upholstery is a rarity) and are usually painted rather than gilded, although what carving there is is often gilded. Country versions are occasionally found in specialist shops in this country.
J+

Sofas

AS in the case of easy chairs, early examples of sofas made little provision for comfortable seating. Some seats were cushioned and a small number used cushioning supported by ropes, in much the same way as early beds were supported. Needless to say, few have survived and we may have underestimated the quantity that existed.

The caned day beds made after 1660 are the earliest survivals in any quantity, and there are not too many Queen Anne and early Georgian examples. After 1750, sofas are measurably more common, usually following fairly closely the designs published at the time, notably Chippendale, Hepplewhite and Sheraton, but it is the Regency that is most typified by elegant classical sofas, usually in rosewood, mahogany or simulated rosewood. The early nineteenth-century system of interior springing resulted in a mass of Victorian sofas in which the structure of the piece is submerged in the deep buttoning. The 'Chesterfield' style and the chaise longue are excellent examples. The twentieth century saw the continuation of the wholly upholstered sofa, many of which are still in use, although in need of respringing.

Most of the examples illustrated are shown on the assumption that re-covering is contemplated. Inexpensive loose covering is an excellent alternative in certain cases, allowing the original coverings to be retained and to some extent protected.

Under £150	**£150–750**	**Over £750**
Unusual Regency	Rosewood (simulated) chaise longue	Arts and Crafts
Articulated day bed	Regency high-backed	Chippendale
Drop end stuffed sofa	Small scroll couch	
Victorian (and later) Chesterfield	Simple Regency chaise longue	
Small window seat	Giltwood sofa	
Chaise longue		
Art Deco chaise longue		
Large padded stool		

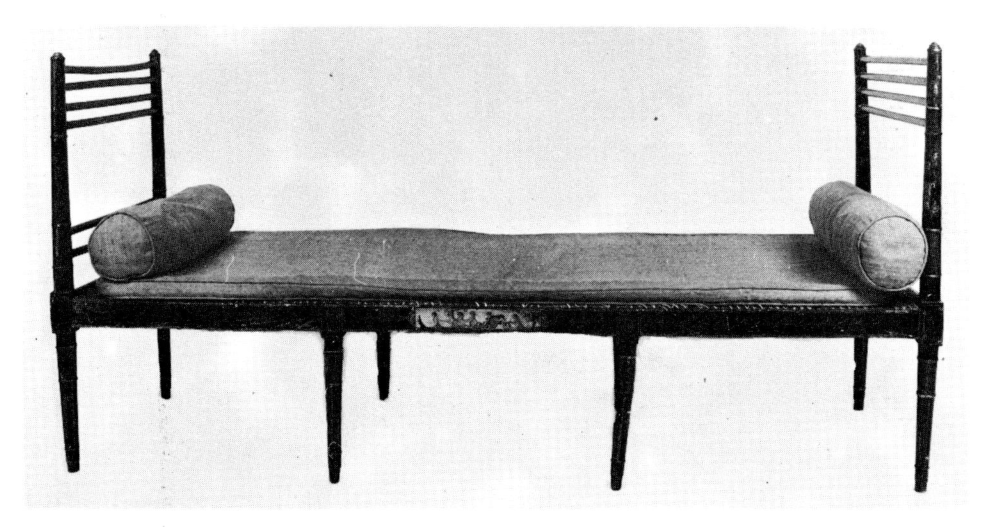

This unusual Regency sofa has painted decoration of putti, juniper leaves and berries along the front rail. The seat is carved and a large squab stuffed with horsehair makes it comfortable – very attractive in the right setting. Note that there is no back to it so it was probably intended to stand against a wall or a wide window.
C+

This extraordinary contrivance is possibly a day bed with some orthopaedic function. But it is comfortable when covered with cushions (the author has tried it out!), so do not be fobbed off by appearances.
B

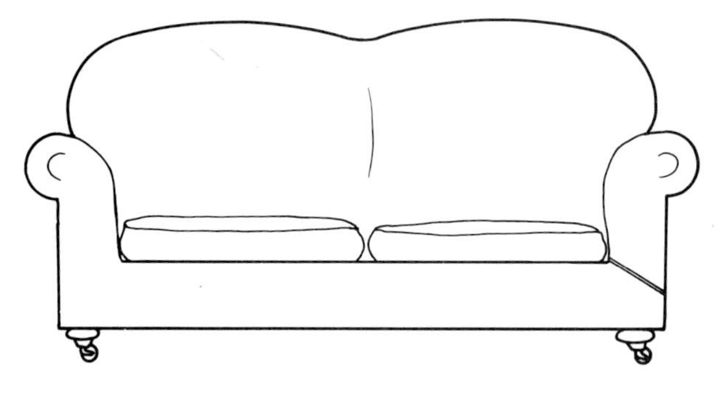

Perhaps the least expensive sofa, and frequently the most comfortable, is the type of early twentieth-century sofa illustrated here. It can be purchased as part of a three-piece suite and loose-covered in a suitable material (most usually a plain linen or a chintz). A desirable feature is a mechanism which allows the arm to drop, enabling the sofa to be used as a day bed.
A

This type of late Victorian chesterfield sofa can seat two or three. Many were covered in leather for smoking rooms. It is best to look for them in sale rooms and large furniture showrooms of the junk yard type; antique shops usually re-cover them which is expensive and gives the buyer no choice.
B

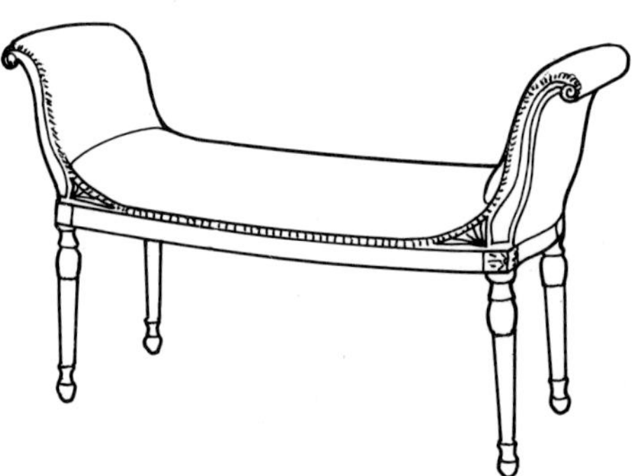

This small upholstered window seat is typical of examples made between about 1775 and 1795. They are very small, intended to sit in a window recess, but they have some use in a modern flat.
C+

A Victorian chaise longue can be acquired inexpensively in an unrestored condition. These are commonly covered in woven black horsehair which is not acceptable today. Re-covering is not cheap, however, and you should be aware of the cost involved. One solution is to embark on the process yourself.
B

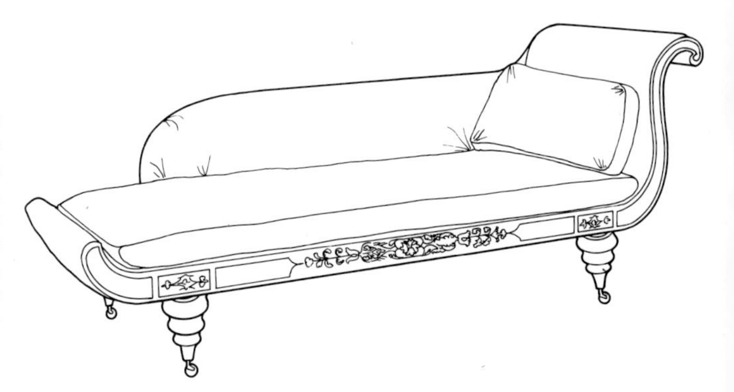

An ottoman is in effect an upholstered box and this 1930s example is in the somewhat unusual form of a sofa. It is really a piece of bedroom furniture but would make a useful addition to an Art Deco sitting room. It retains its original upholstery.
C+

A large padded stool of this sort is much less expensive an enterprise than a sofa. This example has its original upholstery, classic rich Victorian with the elaborate gimp which is so difficult to replace. Usually, however, it will be necessary to embark on some restoration.
C

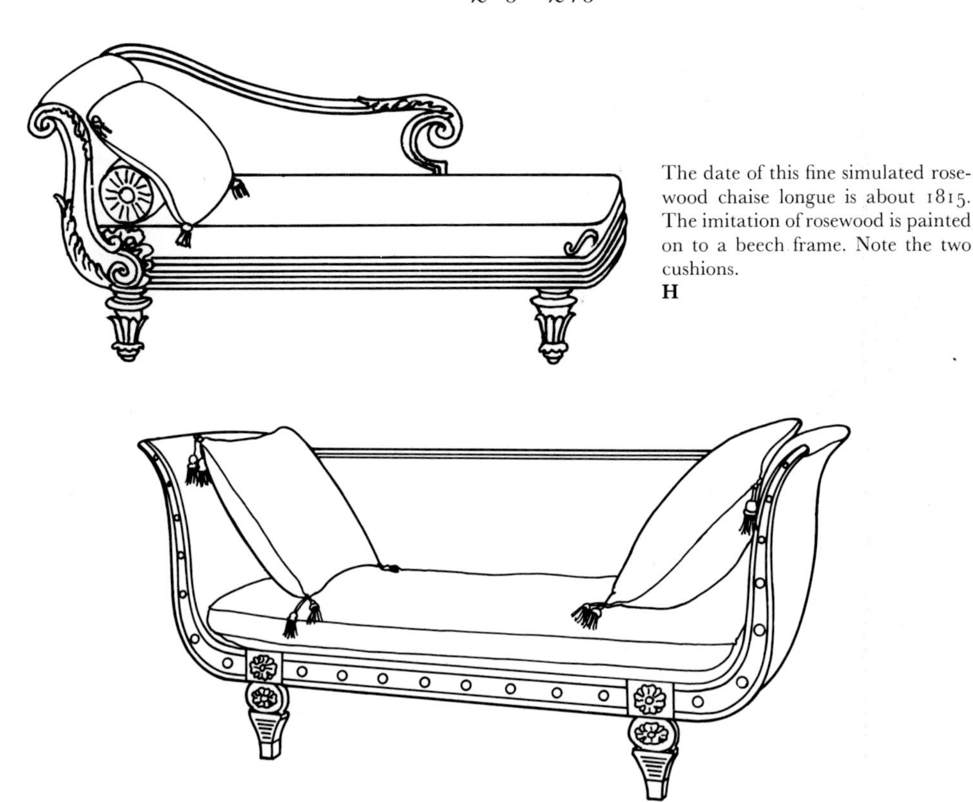

The date of this fine simulated rosewood chaise longue is about 1815. The imitation of rosewood is painted on to a beech frame. Note the two cushions.
H

These high-sided couches, which were popular in Empire France, are stylish pieces which are not as expensive as they deserve. This Regency example is of mahogany with proudly carved feet.
H

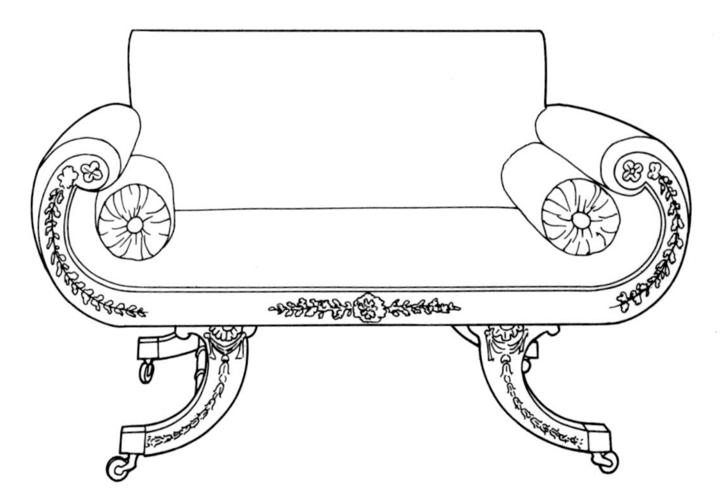

This is a small version of a Regency scroll couch of about 1810. It has sweeping legs on brass castors, and the woodwork is painted black with oak leaf and acorn decoration. This is expensive because of its small size which makes it convenient for a small flat.
G

This simple Regency chaise longue is made of beech but it has been painted to simulate rosewood. You should check to see if paintwork is original or repainted, and if repainted, to what extent. Usually paintwork is damaged, but 'touching up' is a relatively simple task and advice is given in chapter 4. Bear in mind the cost of any necessary reupholstery.
H

Reupholstered gilded sofas reproducing French Louis XV pieces were made in the second half of the nineteenth century. They are gilded beechwood (as are the eighteenth-century prototypes). This example is one of a pair. Usually to be bought in sale rooms, they are by no means expensive.
G

The Arts and Crafts movement produced much furniture of this kind, and designer-attributed examples are very much collected indeed. A. H. Mackmurdo designed this settee, in satinwood (uncharacteristically), for a private house in Cheshire in about 1885. Unattributed pieces tend to go for high prices only if the quality is equally high.
L/M

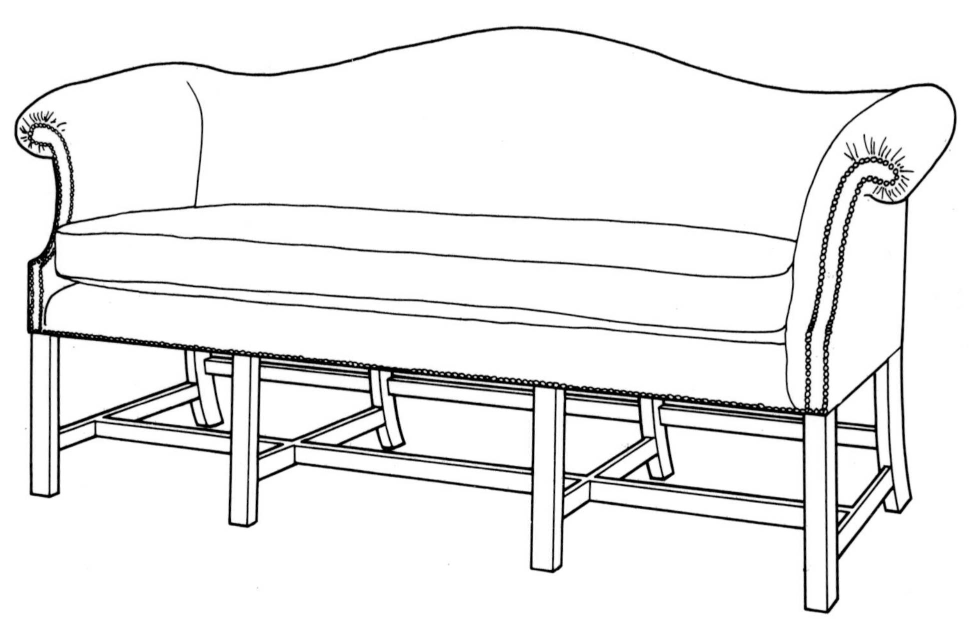

Chippendale's design for a sofa, 1759, is a classic pattern that was used in a simplified form for forty years. It is one of the most popular styles of 'antique' sofa reproduced today. An early period example is expensive and desirable.
K+

Writing Desks and Bureaux

WRITING desks and bureaux are expensive, largely because they are sought not only for use in the home but also by professional and business men who like to set off their offices with the gravity of the antique. So what should you do if your means are limited? If luck is not with you the answer is surely to innovate. A table with a large drawer underneath which perhaps started life as bedroom furniture can be used as a base, and if you can find a small nest of drawers (not too uncommon) or a sequence of boxes to go on top you will have a decorative makeshift arrangement to supplant the expensive desk.

There is no great shortage of desks in the middle range and some of them are most exciting and unusual, but examples of classic grand eighteenth-century pieces can only be found in those good Victorian reproductions available in the better London sale rooms. The best examples are so expensive that you either have to be very well off or much liked by your firm! In the lower and middle areas quite a lot of restoration should be expected, so you should always enquire of the dealer.

Under £150	**£150–750**	**Over £750**
Desk box	Regency kneehole	Bureau
Side table	Davenport	Carlton House desk
Pine 'marriage'	Moorish desk	Chippendale
Wash stand	Country lowboy	
Reproduction lowboy	Schoolmaster's desk	
	Victorian	

A simple desk box is a forerunner of the bureau and its form characterises the bureau as we traditionally know it. They are small and, what is more important, portable. Oak or fruitwoods are commonly used in the construction.
C+

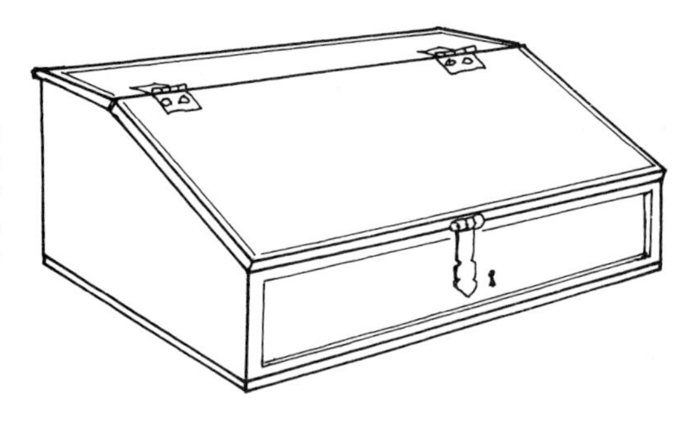

This seventeenth-century oak side table has a large single drawer and is 91 cm (36 in) wide. The stretchers to this example are pegged. A piece without a front stretcher would be more convenient for sitting to write.
C+

In perfect and original condition this typical pine desk would cost well over the lowest price category. But it has had its bracket feet replaced, some drawers have been completely renewed and the handles are not original. This is the kind of extensive restoration that the buyer will have to put up with in the lowest price range. Invariably such pieces of pine have been 'tanked', that is totally immersed in a caustic soda bath, and as a result the pine has a white colour and 'dry' texture.
C

A 'marriage' of a bible box on an oak table makes quite an attractive desk. The carving at the front is nineteenth-century in the style of the seventeenth century. Common sense should tell us that the wear on the stretchers has been simulated; it would be unusual to find genuine signs of wear other than on the main horizontal stretcher.
C+

This pale green painted wash stand with olive green decoration is late eighteenth-century, with nice proportions and two ample drawers. It is 122 cm (48 in) in width, as wide as the average desk, and the shallow splashback can be as convenient as a gallery. This example has simulated bamboo legs.
B/C

This reproduction walnut lowboy was made in the 1920s. It is a good reproduction in that certain period features which are normally absent are present—for example the quarter-veneer on the top. The form of the apron is also typical. But examination shows that the cabriole legs are far too spindly for a period example, and the veneer is too thin. Early veneer is cut by a saw and is about 2.5 mm (1/10 in) thick.
B

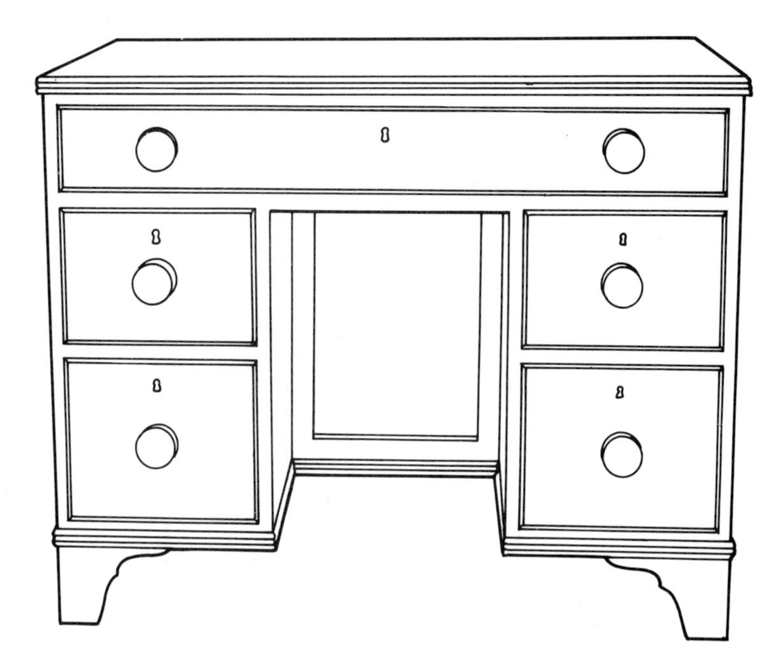

Above: This knee-hole desk is Regency, of about 1820 – an earlier date than might have been supposed. The wood of such desks might be painted to simulate the wavy grain of some light wood or wickerwork and it is lucky if the original paintwork has not been stripped off.
D

Right: A 'Davenport' desk dating from about 1830. Walnut and mahogany examples are more common than rosewood. A small self-raising pigeon-hole section which is called a 'harlequin' is an untypical feature which increases the price by half. They are extraordinarily popular, even though they are not the most convenient of desks.
H+

An interesting late nineteenth-century desk in rosewood, parcel-gilt (employing carved giltwood), in the Moorish taste, was possibly made for Liberty and Company between 1870 and 1880. The serrated arches are most unexpected in English furniture. Although rare it is not excessively expensive.
G

This attractive country lowboy is in fruitwood with a large single drawer. The square cabriole legs are a typical country feature, both crude and appealing. It is probably about 1730, but these examples are often difficult to date.
G

A well made oak schoolmaster's desk from the second half of the eighteenth century would clearly be less convenient than either a bureau or a flat-topped desk, but this is reflected in the price.
E

This late Victorian walnut pedestal writing desk (about 1880), has a distinctive figure to the well matched veneer. It is made by Maple and Company. Victorian pieces, when marked, are most commonly stamped with the maker's name on the edge of one of the top drawers.
H+

Left: This plain mahogany bureau fitted with small drawers and pigeon holes dates from about 1780. The bureau developed from the scriptor, but came into its recognisable form by the end of the seventeenth century. A shell inlay on the outside of the fall flap usually indicates that the piece is a late nineteenth-century copy – nonetheless desirable – of a Sheraton original.

J+

Bottom: Despite its simplicity this is a most expensive example of a partner's desk. It is plain Chippendale period of the finest quality wood, with a writing slope set into the leather top.

M+

Below: The famous 'Carlton House' type of desk is found in mahogany and rosewood, often with extensive satinwood panels. The expression has no proven connection with the Carlton House of the Prince Regent. They were made from about 1795 to 1815 and are among the most elegant pieces of Georgian furniture.

M+

Bookcases

BOOKCASES really mean 'shelving', for most people use a bookcase only in part for books, leaving space for displaying small collections of porcelain, glass or other objects of art. One solution is merely to buy shelving which can rest against the wall (preferably anchored to it), but the cost of basic materials for such work is quite high and many antique bookcases compare favourably in price. Small bookcases can be purchased for reasonable sums in junk shops (and even good antique shops). There is a large number of bamboo bookcases available, despite recent interest in that material. Small glazed cabinets are an excellent choice for collections of valuable books as open bookcases allow dust and dirt to settle.

In the more expensive categories, bookcase sections are often found attached to bureaux or chests. They can be outstandingly expensive, but untypical examples can go for smaller sums. The large breakfront bookcases are not rare, but they are extremely expensive. Their architectural proportions usually dictate the room they go into, most having originally been designed for large libraries in country houses. It is rather a sad state of affairs that these bookcases should today frequently be illuminated from the inside to display a large dinner service – decorative maybe, but a misuse.

Early bookcases are rare. Book collections were scarce and not large and were kept in cupboards called presses. The first recognisable bookcases, then also called presses, are those made for Samuel Pepys by 'Sympson, the joyner' and now in Magdalene College, Cambridge.

Under £150	**£150–750**	**Over £750**
Eight examples of 19th and 20th-century bookcases	Victorian waist high	Pepysian
	Large Victorian	Hepplewhite
	Georgian stepped	Gothic
	Small library bookcase	Simple gothic

A number of these small Victorian bookcases are available for relatively little outlay. This example in mahogany, about 1860, has rather better proportions than most. It is 88 cm (35 in) wide; always check the height against that of your ceiling!
B

Below: An English mahogany bookcase with three shelves and glazed doors dating from about 1860. Note the leather flaps which hang down from the shelves. Their purpose is to prevent dust accumulating on the top edges of the stored books and they are a nice period feature.
C

Above left: This type of simple bookcase in pitch pine is likely to have come from a church vestry and to date from about 1860. It is about 1 metre (40 in) in width.
B

Above right: This type of bookcase, made in considerable numbers in the last quarter of the nineteenth century, can still be found in many small antique shops, and even in junk shops. They were made in varying qualities, using oak, mahogany and even stained deals. Although the latter are the cheapest they are often prone to damage and worming.
B/C

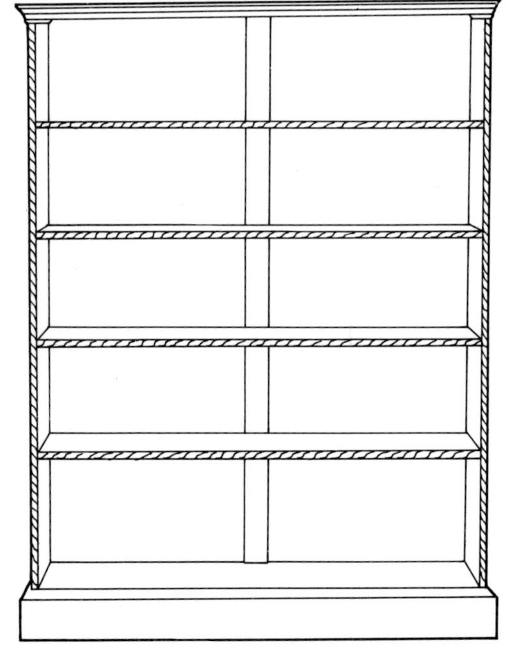

Many bookcases were veneered and have subsequently had that veneer removed to expose the pine carcass. Similarly many painted bookcases have been stripped in a caustic solution to expose the carcass, again usually pine. These are not outstandingly expensive or difficult to find.
A

Revolving bookcases on this principle date from the middle of the nineteenth century although this example is early twentieth century. It can stand in the centre of a room and is extremely capacious. Smaller revolving bookcases are found which stand on top of tables and early examples are even made of bamboo.
C *Bamboo* **C+** *Other materials*

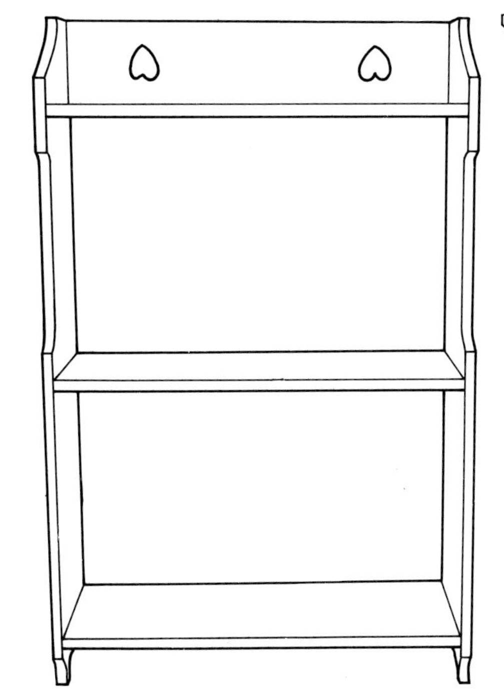

This illustration shows a bookshelf of the kind that is found extensively and inexpensively in more general antique shops. It is in oak and the inverted heart shapes which enable it to be hung are typical Arts and Crafts motifs.
A/B

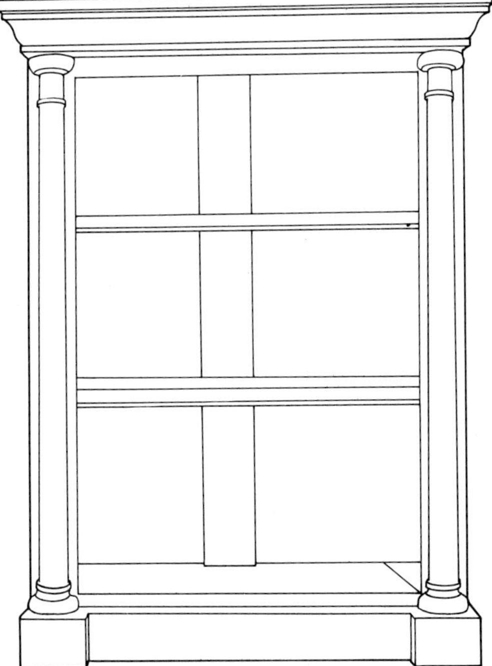

This good small mahogany bookcase with columns has architectural proportions unusual for a small piece. It dates from about 1840. This is most suitable for a small flat or to set in the bay between two windows.
B/C

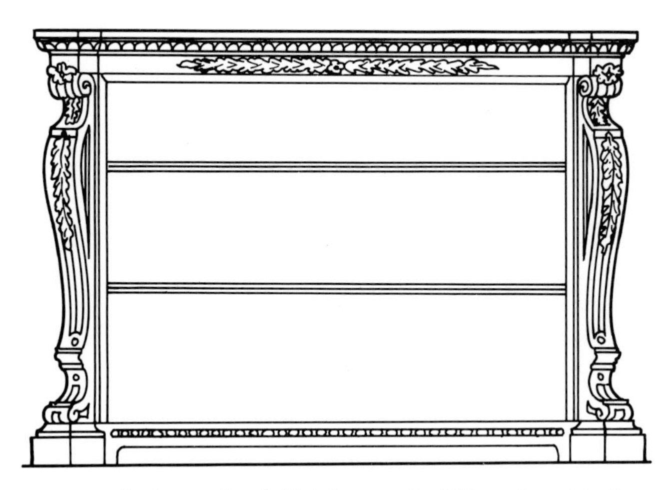

Waist high bookcases are usually cheaper than full height examples. This version, of the first years of the reign of Queen Victoria, continues to show the finer classical lines of the first part of the century, even though it would have been made by mechanical methods. Veneer and applied carving should be checked for condition.
E/F

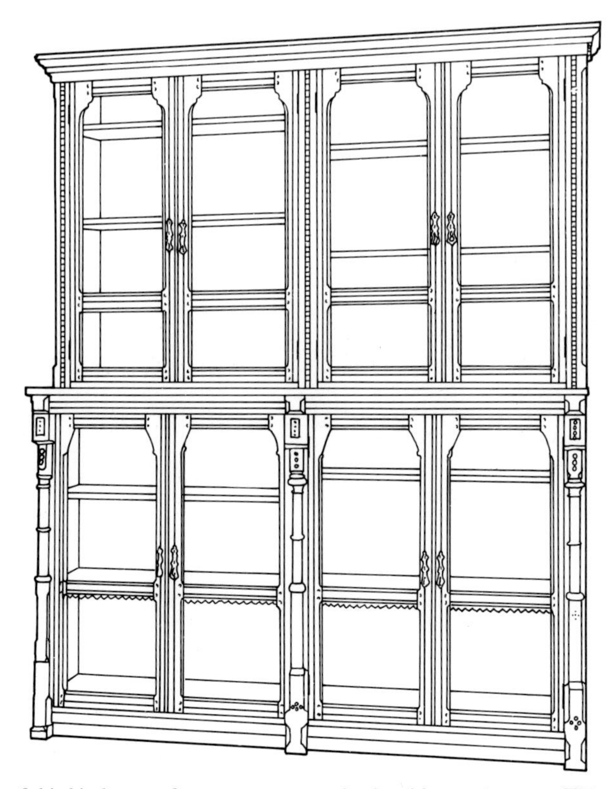

Victorian furniture of this kind was a few years ago completely without advocates. This example in oak is of robust construction and in its detail is reminiscent of the work of the well known Victorian designer, Bruce Talbert. Today the finer examples reach top prices, but sometimes lesser pieces fail to reach their reserves at auctions.
F/G

Note the carrying handles on this late eighteenth-century bookcase. It has a small drawer beneath and is in satinwood with ebony stringing. These pieces which are small and have characteristic stepped-back shelves are ideal for flats and fit well in corridors and between windows. About 1795.
H

This William IV square bookcase in rosewood (about 1838) is a good example of library furniture. Although scarce they need not be excessively expensive. William IV furniture frequently has damage to the veneer; a rosewood veneer is less vulnerable than mahogany.
G

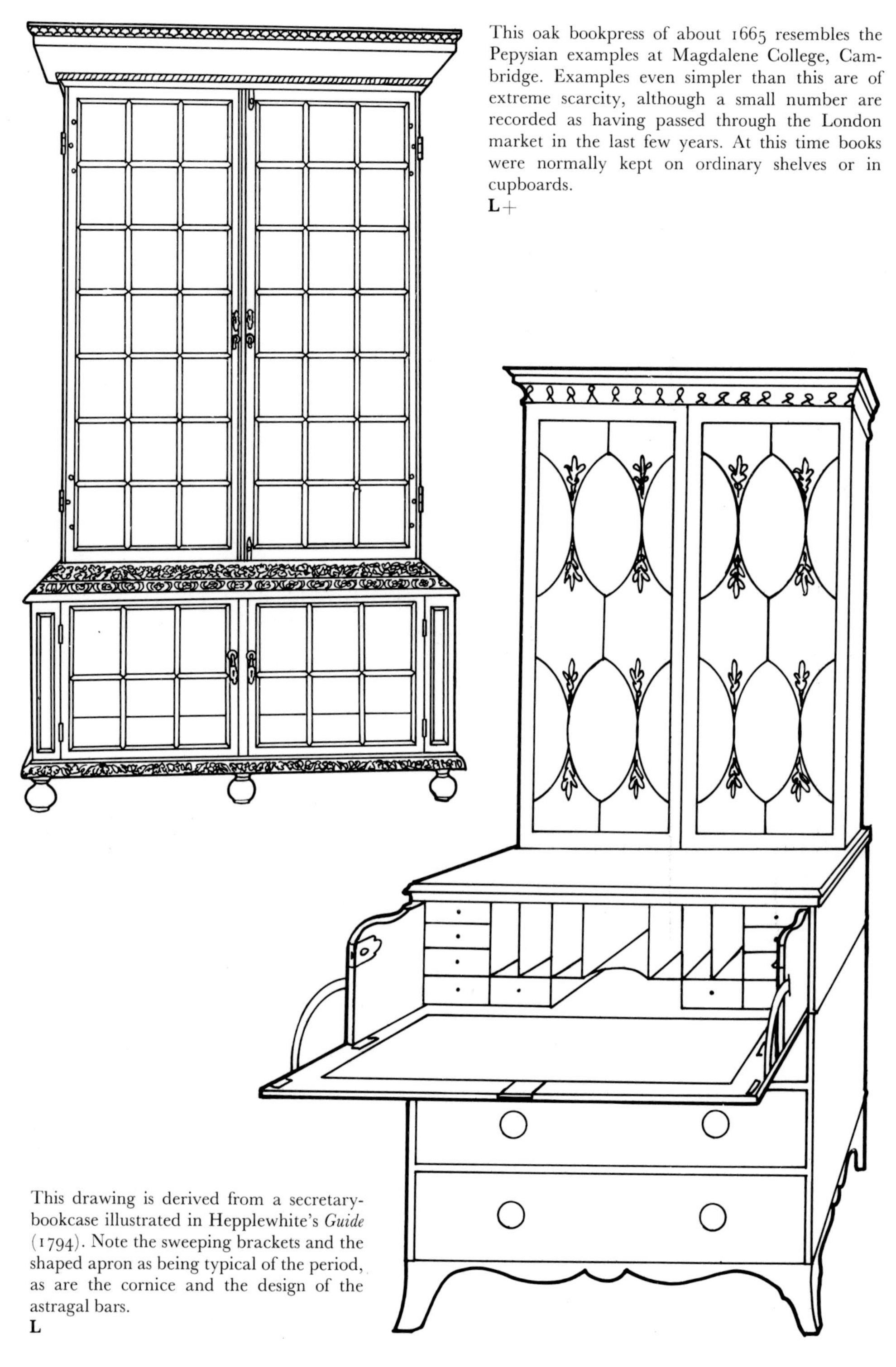

This oak bookpress of about 1665 resembles the Pepysian examples at Magdalene College, Cambridge. Examples even simpler than this are of extreme scarcity, although a small number are recorded as having passed through the London market in the last few years. At this time books were normally kept on ordinary shelves or in cupboards.
L+

This drawing is derived from a secretary-bookcase illustrated in Hepplewhite's *Guide* (1794). Note the sweeping brackets and the shaped apron as being typical of the period, as are the cornice and the design of the astragal bars.
L

A rare and fine early nineteenth-century Gothic bookcase shows a fairly sophisticated assimilated understanding of the purer Gothic. Earlier examples of this type are rather free and romantic interpretations which are unmistakably Georgian.
M+

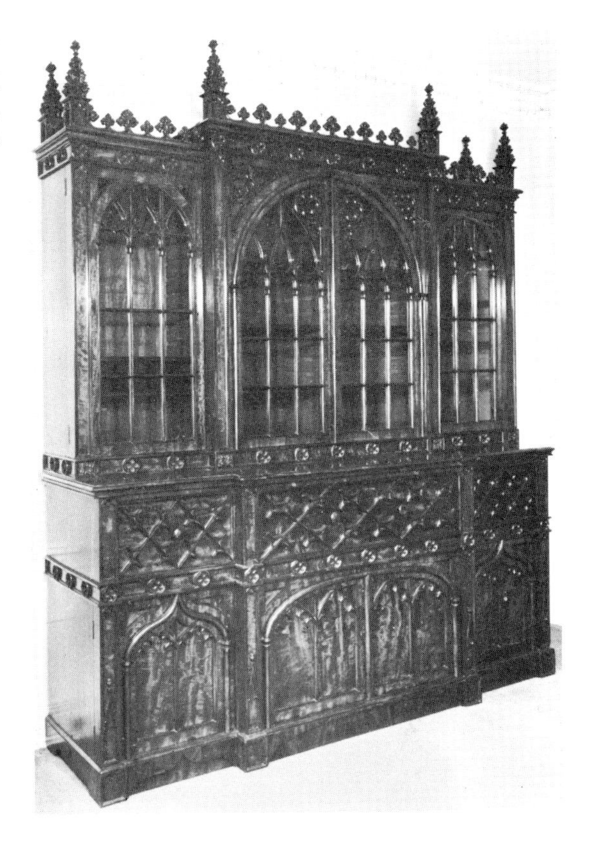

This is a good and typical example of a mahogany breakfront bookcase in the Gothic taste, about 1795. Even when simple these are among the most expensive pieces of furniture. Beware of over restoration and outright 'fakes'.
L

Beds

IN the nineteenth century the brass bed was responsible for the loss of many older beds, on the ground that wooden beds with old stuffed mattresses harboured vermin. This may well have been true, but wooden beds were made (usually for the grander type of purchaser) at all times throughout the nineteenth century. It was Sir Ambrose Heal's designs for wooden beds at the turn of the century that resulted in the demise of the metal bed.

The problem in buying a bed is the question of the mattress. It is possible to have a mattress made to fit any bed, but this is a considerable expense so it is of the first importance to make certain that a standard size mattress can be fitted. If the dealer assures you of this make sure he will take the bed back if it does not prove to be the case.

Apart from a small number of specialist dealers in beds, the best place to buy is the sale room (though the mattress problem is more acute). The average antique dealer does not usually keep beds, largely because of the space they take up. When a dealer does have them they are usually dismantled at the back of the shop, having been purchased in a house clearance, and he is frequently only too happy to be rid of them.

Old beds were originally 'roped' in a net pattern and stuffed mattresses were heaped upon them. If you propose to do away with this scheme do not interfere with the structure. Interior sprung mattresses can be had to fit over the bed-frame without causing it damage. The fairly high cost of early beds justifies this expense.

Under £150	**£150–750**	**Over £750**
Painted provincial	Oak stump	Hepplewhite
Cot	Brass campaign	Fine four poster
Cheap brass and cast iron	American style	
Commercial Victorian/Edwardian	Half tester	
Victorian stump	'Four poster'	
	Panelled bed	

Only the head is shown of this early nineteenth-century provincial painted bed. It is European, possibly Spanish, though the naive quality of the painting is reminiscent of that found on many American examples of the early nineteenth century. It is 122 cm (48 in) wide.
C+

A mid-Victorian child's cot is still a practical alternative and is only marginally more expensive than a good modern cot. In light-coloured mahogany, about 122 cm (48 in) long, it has caned removable sides and in addition can be completely dismantled.
C+

Elaborate brass beds are now expensive whereas iron beds, even when polished, are inexpensive. Between the two are iron beds which utilise brass in the decoration and these are still within the pocket of the less well off. The head rail illustrated is 157 cm (54 in) wide.
B

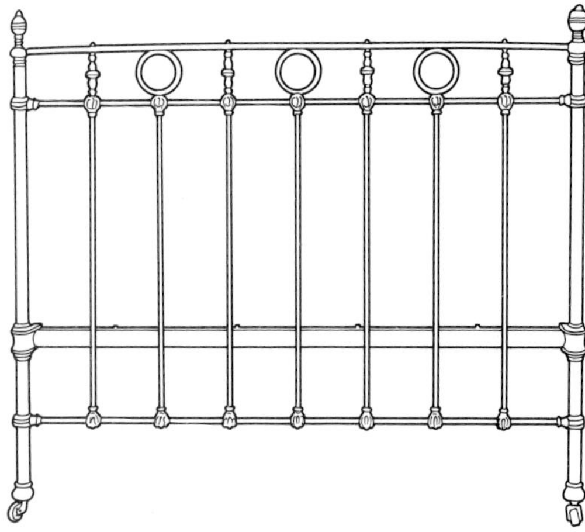

Below: A late Victorian/Edwardian mahogany bed is probably the cheapest buy at a saleroom or repository. With vertical slats in the head rest and at the foot, they are found as single or double beds and were intended originally to have feather and horsehair mattresses. Often they are inlaid with satinwood banding.
A

This is a Victorian stump bedstead design of about 1859 by W. A. Smee and Sons. Most nineteenth-century beds had railing at the foot, not a popular feature today. This Victorian example, even with no offending rail, can still be had for little outlay.
A

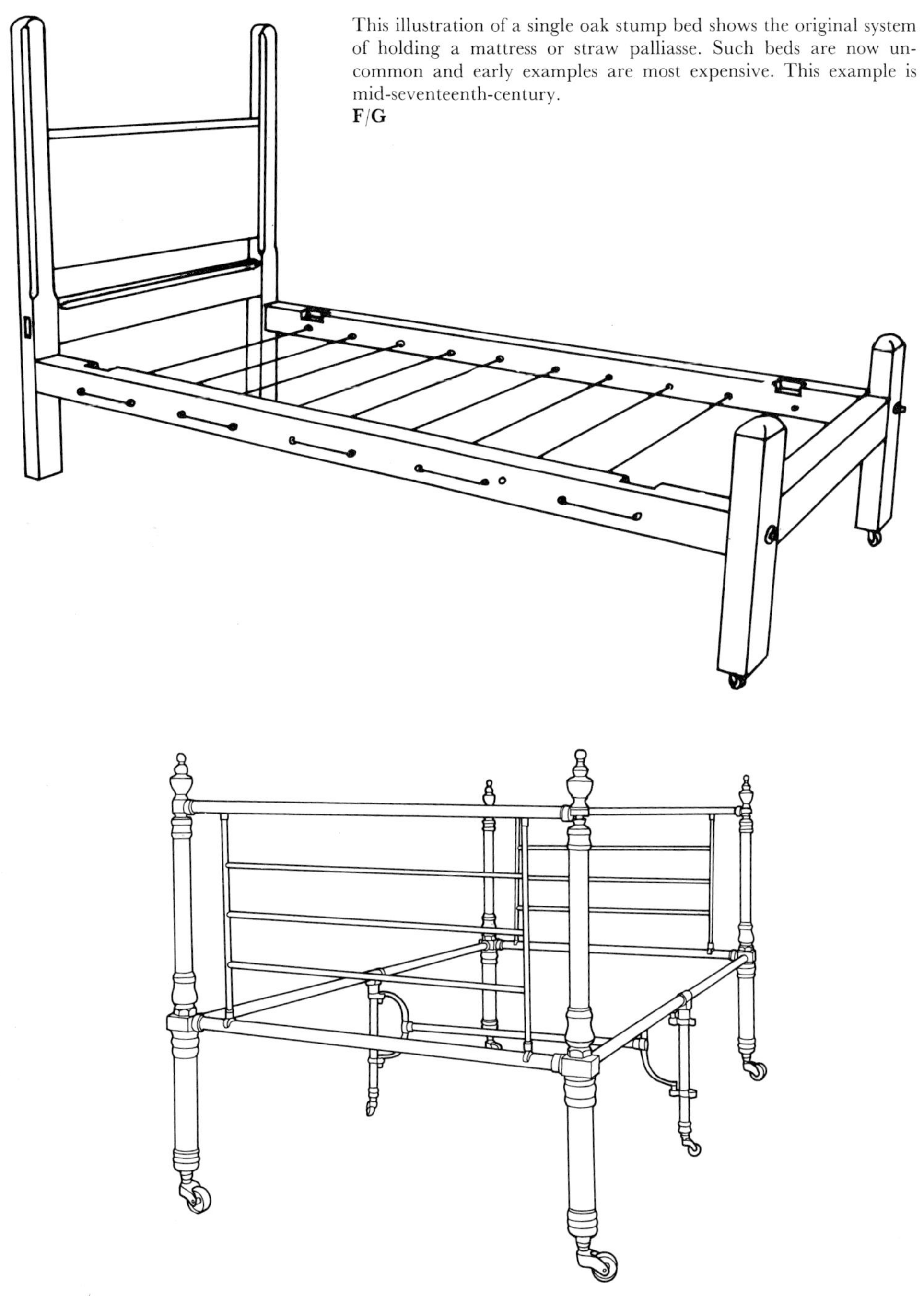

This illustration of a single oak stump bed shows the original system of holding a mattress or straw palliasse. Such beds are now uncommon and early examples are most expensive. This example is mid-seventeenth-century.
F/G

This type of fine quality early nineteenth-century brass campaign bed was made so as to dismantle with ease and speed. The quality of later mass-produced pieces deteriorated. Look out for iron beds which have been brass-bound: if the iron rusts (as often happens) the brass binding splits. Also, for ease, buy your brass bed lacquered with clear varnish: it will save endless hours of polishing.
G/H

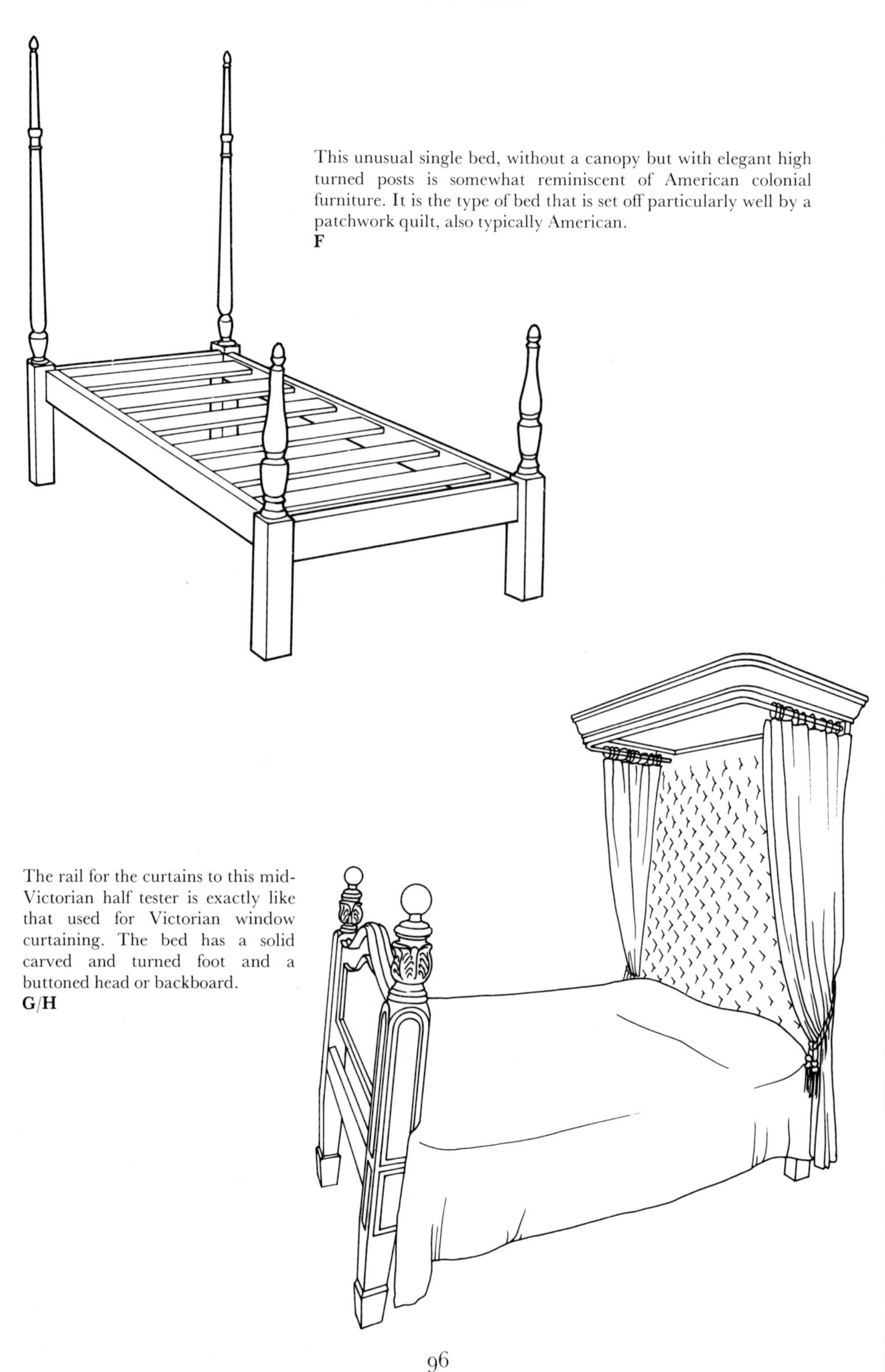

This unusual single bed, without a canopy but with elegant high turned posts is somewhat reminiscent of American colonial furniture. It is the type of bed that is set off particularly well by a patchwork quilt, also typically American.
F

The rail for the curtains to this mid-Victorian half tester is exactly like that used for Victorian window curtaining. The bed has a solid carved and turned foot and a buttoned head or backboard.
G/H

This early Victorian 'four poster' with turned mahogany columns only has two posts as such. As with many so-called four posters, a backboard usually serves instead of the two back legs, everything being united by a tester or canopy.
H

An eighteenth-century panelled bed may well have been constructed out of surplus panelling. They are not uncommon, need not be expensive and are interesting examples of cottage furniture.
G

This classical eighteenth-century bed, in the Hepplewhite manner, dates from about 1785. The cornice is painted with ribbons and flowers and the mahogany posts are octagonal, set upon slim reeded urns. The structure is often held together by bolts through the legs, concealed by plates.
L

Below: A good early English oak posted bed dating from the first half of the sixteenth century. Many examples are to be found (slightly later in date) but they have nearly all been assembled later than it initially appears. Much carving is nineteenth-century in date although the structure may be old. Despite extensive restoration, prices are very high.
M+

Chests

THE chest is one of the essential requirements for storing clothes and other belongings. It still holds its own against the 'fitted' cupboard and is often extremely cheap. We tend to think of it as being a box with about five drawers, three long and two short, and in mahogany. No doubt this may well describe the majority of chests of drawers but the selection illustrated is much wider. Basically what is required is a few sliding drawers, but an example of a more unusual 'chest' is the travelling trunk shown on page 102 which adequately serves as a blanket chest or a store for children's toys. Furthermore, the chest is not just a piece of bedroom furniture: it is valuable wherever it is placed and can enhance the appearance of a sitting room far more effectively than a cabinet.

Rare pieces need not be expensive. Size is one of the most important factors and it is the early eighteenth-century small walnut bachelor's chest that is perhaps the most expensive piece available. A large Victorian chest of drawers, veneered in mahogany can still, with luck, be picked up in a country auction for a few pounds. Painted pine or deal chests are usually the cheapest. Although you can strip off the paint, ask yourself if it is really necessary: perhaps the original paintwork has an appeal you may have overlooked at first? At any rate, there are more chests of drawers on the market than anything else, with the exception of chairs, so you have a wide choice with which to mesmerise yourself.

Under £150	**£150–750**	**Over £750**
Hepplewhite style, 19th-century	Italian	Chest on chest
Shop fittings	Bow front	Bachelor chest
Georgian pine	Pine chest on stand	Walnut
Early 19th-century		Chippendale period
Trunk		
Commode		

A late nineteenth-century mahogany chest of drawers in imitation of the Hepplewhite style is still available for sums towards the upper end of the cheapest price category. This is a good copy, though the ebony inlay just above the top drawer is untypical of the Hepplewhite style. The keyholes (escutcheons) have ivory inlaid surrounds.
C

A chest of drawers like this has probably been taken from a well fitted Victorian shop, most likely a chemist as the shelves have a marble slab on top. The original mass handles survive. It is a most useful contrivance for storage in a kitchen or a study, or indeed anywhere. Nowadays they are much collected but not excessively expensive.
B/C

This is a simple late Georgian stripped pine chest of drawers, in good condition with no restoration. There are turned wooden handles and the proportions are carefully balanced, even in a simple country example like this one.
B

This is a plain mahogany chest of drawers, about 1840, of a good large size with a capacious bottom drawer. The handles are turned mahogany. This example is deceptively early in appearance.
C+

As well as an excellent storage box, a trunk serves as a stylish ottoman or blanket chest. This one has a domed top (less expensive than a flat-topped chest) and is made of stamped leather with applied wooden splats.
A

This late Georgian commode has been converted (some time ago) into a small chest of drawers. The balance of the drawers at the front is disproportionate but this is a useful piece of furniture for a small flat.
B

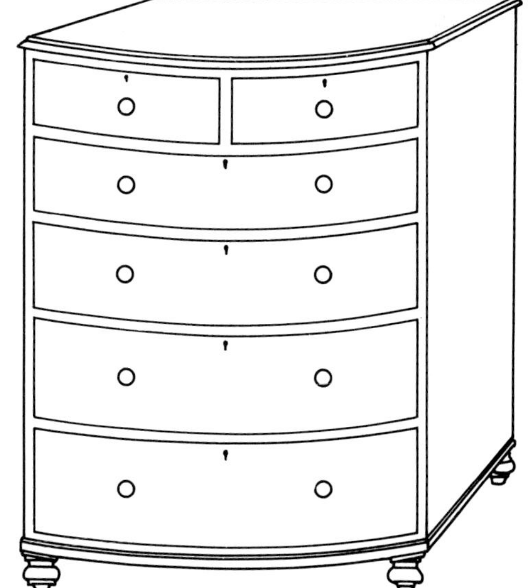

Above: The top of this eighteenth-century Italian chest is painted to imitate marble. The ground paint is white with bright flower and foliage decorations. Painted decoration ages rather more noticeably than any other. This piece has not been restored, although it has been cleaned of surface dirt. Restoration of painted woods is problematical: it is usually better not to embark on the task unless the decoration has ceased to be recognisable.
F

Above right: From about 1770–1850, simple tall mahogany chests of drawers were made in great numbers. They are usually well made, particularly the earlier ones, and the most usual clue to quality lies in details such as inlay, handles (beware replacements) and locks.
D–G

Right: If a chest on stand were in walnut it would be extremely expensive and would date from about 1690–1720. This country pine example, almost certainly a copy, is measurably later (about 1800). There are also American examples from the middle of the eighteenth century. Undoubtedly this chest would have been painted to simulate a wood such as mahogany. Although uncommon it is not unreasonably expensive.
H

This chest on chest, or tallboy, has well matched walnut veneers. It is George I, about 1714–20. The corners to the upper stage are canted, or chamfered, and fluted and there is the rarer feature of an inlaid sunburst in the lower section.
L

Bachelor chests are very small – seldom more than 72 cm (28 in) long and 23 cm (9 in) deep – and very expensive. Some less usual examples are in solid walnut and not veneered, dating from about 1715–20. The top lifts over as a flap which is supported by two draw slides.
L

Nowadays this fine William and Mary chest of drawers, dating from about 1700, is quite a rare piece. It is veneered in highly figured walnut, with ebony stringing. Note the half round mouldings around the drawers (too early a period for cock beading) and the bun feet (which are usually replacements).
K

This is a low mid-eighteenth-century chest of drawers in mahogany. A plain straight-grained mahogany was much sought after by Chippendale and his contemporaries; highly elaborate 'flame' figured mahogany was also much used, but the internal weakness of burr woods made them difficult to work with.
K

Occasional Tables

THERE is no end to what we can mean by the phrase 'occasional table'. In the seventeenth century when furniture was much prized, functional pieces were important. What was needed was a large table to work on and smaller tables to carry from room to room as occasion demanded. There can surely be little doubt that the three-legged 'cricket' table had a great variety of functions. In the eighteenth century, tables were designed for a specific purpose and we must gather from records and pictures that most were kept out of the room, or to the side of it, until the *occasion* arose for them to be required. Work tables, tea-urn stands, coaching tables, games tables, butlers' trays, tea tables and card tables are just a few examples – the list could be extended indefinitely. This wide range stimulated a consumer boom and throughout the nineteenth century small tables continued to have specific functions invented for them.

Many expressions have been hallowed by use but leave one mystified as to what occasion prompted their adoption. A Pembroke table, for instance, is occasional, but one cannot say for what purpose. Even the somewhat unreliable evidence that they were first made for Lady Pembroke gives us no clue. Also included are a few tables whose use was more architectural than immediately practical. Examination of interior designs reveals console tables, pier tables and side tables that remained in their place as adjuncts of a pleasing scheme of decoration.

Under £150	**£150–750**	**Over £750**
Pub	Side table	Satinwood 18th-century
Butler's	Tea caddy table	George II tip-top
Pembroke	Coaching table	
Dumb waiter		
Victorian tea		
Victorian centre		
Cricket		
Small round		
Bamboo		

Above left: Vast numbers of these cast iron pub tables were made. This example of about 1870 has been sandblasted to present a brilliant metallic surface (which is difficult to maintain). Other examples were painted or stoved.
B

Left: A butler's tray was never intended to remain in a room: the butler would remove it when he had performed his duties. As a drinks tray it has no equal as it can be carried from room to room. A few years ago these cost less than five pounds, and even though they are ten times as expensive today they are still good value. This example in mahogany dates from the 1830s.
B

Left: Pembroke tables must have been made in great quantities as a large number of them survive. This is an English example in mahogany, dating from about 1820. Usually they are in good condition, but it is always wise to ask whether the table tops and flaps are original. Often the legs have been cut down, but the normal height of such a table is 74–76.5 cm (29–30 in).
C+

Top: An alternative to a three-tiered mahogany dumb waiter, which is now expensive, is this Victorian example in brass with mahogany tiers. It is smaller than the more usual type. These are used for display purposes today and are sought after.
B

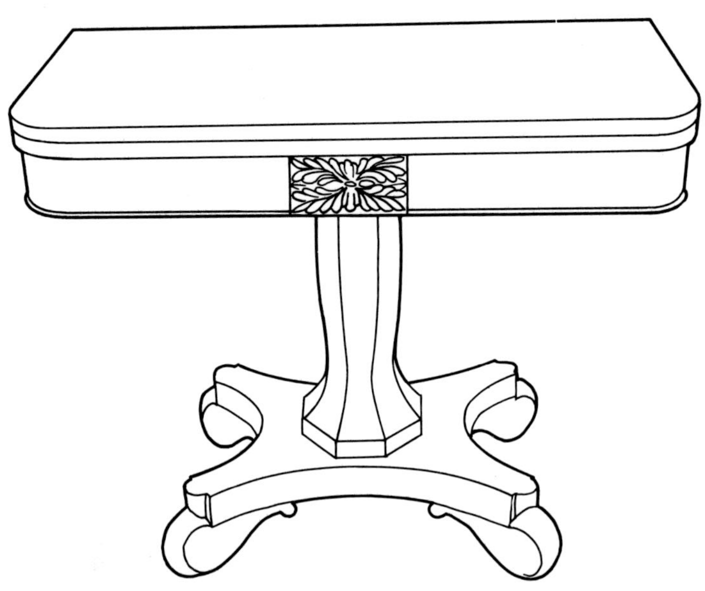

This type of early Victorian rosewood tea table, of about 1840, was made in considerable numbers, the detail on the frieze being machine-carved. The veneer on such pieces is surprisingly vulnerable. This table could equally well be a card table, with a baize cloth set into the table top.
C

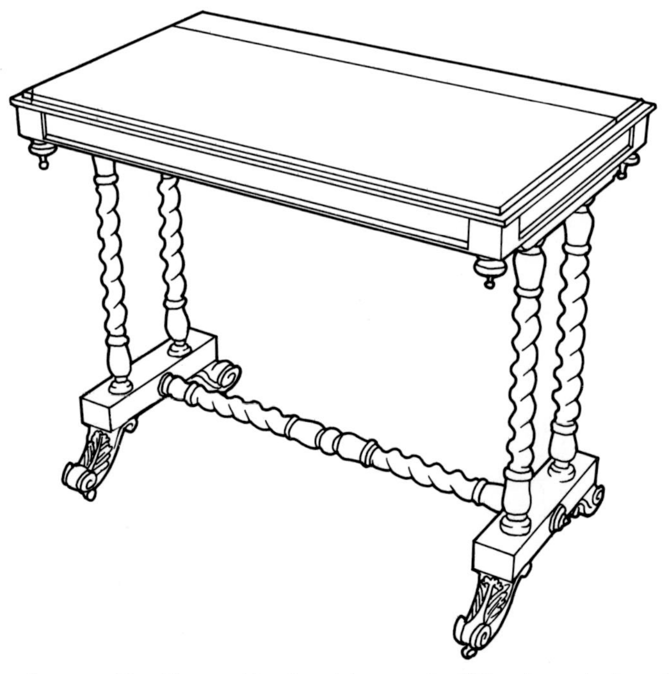

A Victorian rosewood centre table with turned legs is a plain example of Victorian revivalism; the barley sugar twist of the legs is a feature of furniture of the second half of the seventeenth century. (It is interesting to note that the historicism of Victorian commercial furniture was often markedly inaccurate.) The highly polished rosewood top is matched by brightly varnished legs, which in many cases are stained to resemble rosewood.
B

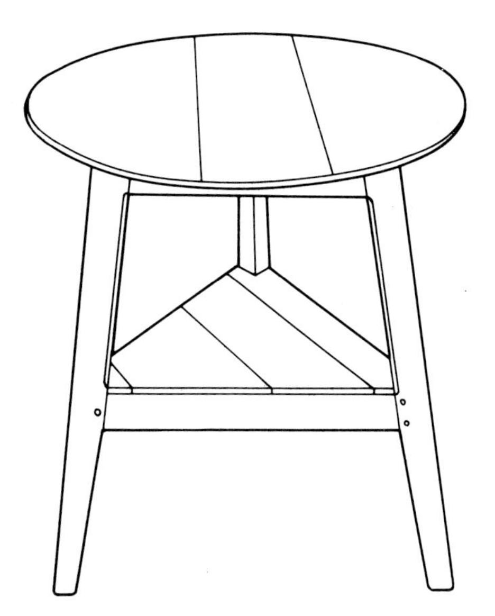

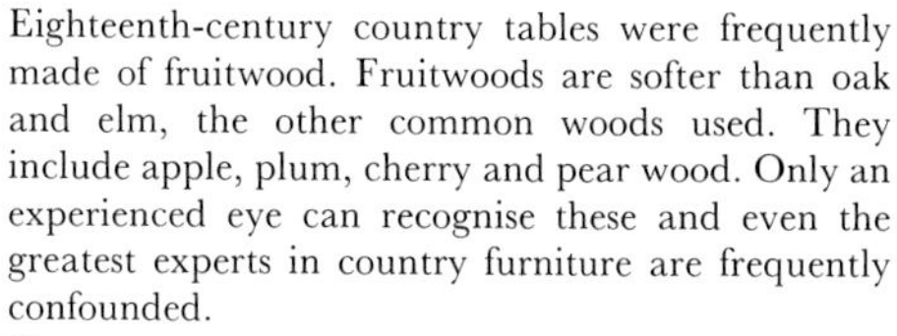

Eighteenth-century country tables were frequently made of fruitwood. Fruitwoods are softer than oak and elm, the other common woods used. They include apple, plum, cherry and pear wood. Only an experienced eye can recognise these and even the greatest experts in country furniture are frequently confounded.
C

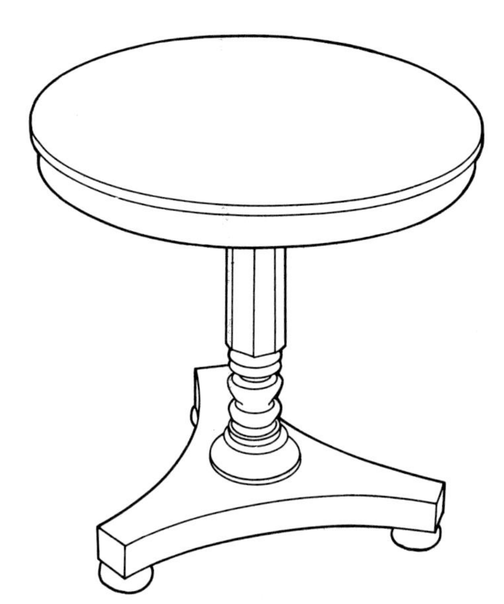

If you come across a piece of furniture with V.R. and a royal crown stamped upon it, do not be tempted to think that it was necessarily the personal property of Queen Victoria. The stamp on this mahogany table denotes that it was government property, probably one of many used in official buildings. It is 74 cm (29 in) high, with a turned column on a circular base and bun feet, and it dates from about 1845.
B

This bamboo table is English, dating from the nineteenth century. A certain type of bamboo, called 'tortoiseshell', has a mottled appearance. It is very often encountered on bamboo furniture made in the West, although many English-made examples are plain. Plain bamboo was used for furniture made in the Orient for export to Europe.
A

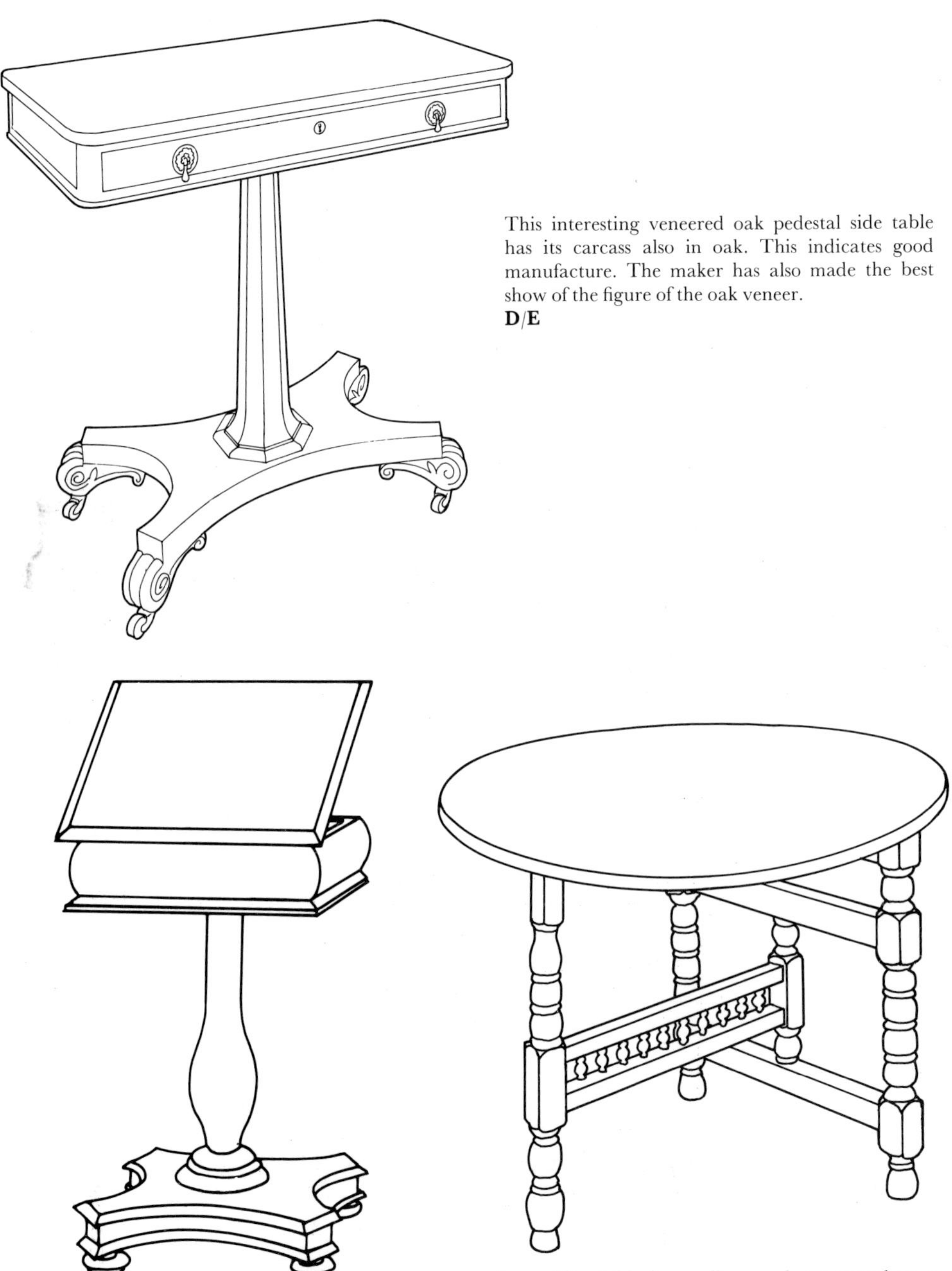

This interesting veneered oak pedestal side table has its carcass also in oak. This indicates good manufacture. The maker has also made the best show of the figure of the oak veneer.
D/E

This type of furniture could be used for many purposes, for example as a teapoy in which tea caddies and glass mixing bowls were kept, or as a sewing box, well fitted with small drawers for silks etc. They are quite common but fairly expensive as conveniently small and often highly decorative.
F/G

A coaching table is usually round, supported on a gateleg action which allowed it to be folded away flat and carried in a coach. The good seventeenth-century example shown here is very sophisticated, in walnut with elaborately turned legs. More rudimentary examples are more common and less expensive.
H+

Painted furniture rarely survives intact as it does in this excellent late eighteenth-century tripod table. It is in satinwood, crossbanded with tulipwood. The octagonal top is painted with a richly coloured border of swags of flowers.
J+

A classic of its kind is a George II mahogany pie-crust edged tripod table. It is very fine quality and beautifully carved, dating from about 1755. Beware the carving; spurious work is shown up by a shallowness in its profile (see page 30).
L

Dressers and Sideboards

THE side 'board' is a piece of furniture of great antiquity: it stood originally at the side of a room subsidiary to the main 'board' – the dining or refectory table. Functions were diverse. In a dining room it became a vehicle of display as well as a practical holdall and dispenser of wines, food, silver and glass. In the kitchen the equivalent is the 'dresser', literally a place where food was 'dressed', or the last stages of preparation were carried out. On it dishes, spices, ladles and other essentials were racked on shelves, when the dresser was equipped with racks, or stored underneath in large drawers.

Today sideboards are both desirable and expensive. In the sense of the more formal conception in mahogany made from 1750 onwards they are, it is true, numerous. But demand exceeds availability and they are continually rising in price. This is true even of reproductions. One point to note is that most of these sideboards have been 'converted' – not fundamentally, but the two drawers at either end have usually been altered. One was usually a lead lined 'cellarette' drawer; today drawers have often been changed into cupboard doors, the lead removed and shelves inserted to hold silver or napkins. Green baize interiors often conceal restoration.

The dresser is equally a rarity because a more informal style of living makes them much in demand. Oak dressers, piled high with redundant Victorian serving dishes and plates brought home from abroad are today more commonly found in sitting rooms than in kitchens.

What is left? Some Victorian sideboards remain inexpensive; some chiffoniers are good value for money; pine is a sure standby; and a successful alternative is a Victorian marble-topped washstand – they are outstandingly practicable as they usually have splashbacks to protect walls. No doubt some other alternative will offer itself once you start to look around.

Under £150	**£150–750**	**Over £750**
Thirties'	Victorian chiffonier	Oak 18th-century dresser
Wash stand	Food hutch	Oak 17th-century court cupboard
19th-century dresser	19th-century dresser	Georgian sideboard
Reproduction sideboard	Bow front sideboard	
Victorian sideboard		

Right: Some modern sideboards are of good quality and simple lines. Specimens from Heal's and Maples' in the twenties and thirties can be excellent value and of solid construction. They are sometimes found in repositories and can be very inexpensive.
B/C

Centre: A Victorian marble topped wash stand can still be found with ease, but gradually they are creeping up in price. The marble top is an excellent surface for hot dishes, and if the piece were required in a kitchen would represent an excellent preparation surface. Some examples can be found which simulate a marble top; these are less expensive, but because they are pine underneath, they are often stripped. It is often worth asking a dealer who specialises in stripped pine to set aside such things before he strips them.
B

Below: A cheap nineteenth-century dresser can look very successful, particularly when a pine set of shelves is placed above it. This is a simple example of the machine made cottage variety, in pine, with turned wooden handles to the drawers. Although humble, they are becoming expensive and need to be sought out, the best place to find them being the stripped pine market.
C

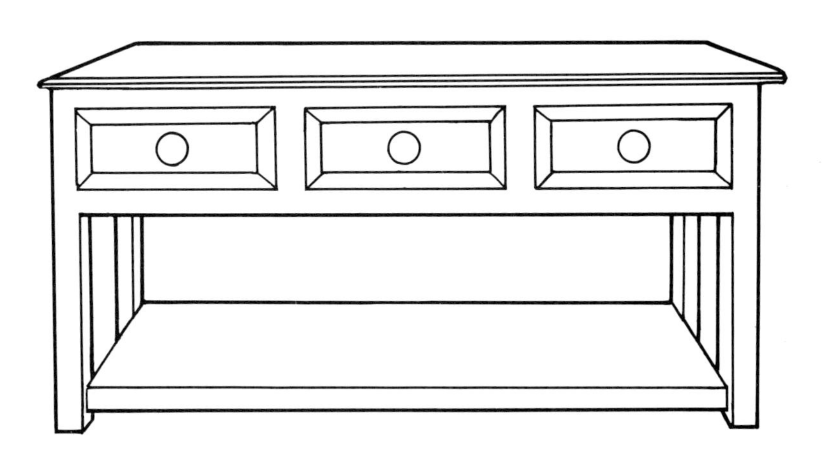

Reproduction sideboards of the kind illustrated vary in quality, but some can be quite inexpensive. They imitate very simply late Georgian examples and date from the latter years of the nineteenth century, although the majority of the examples sold on the market are from the twenties and thirties. They are still being made. Quality varies so much that they cannot confidently be recommended. Look out in particular for the depth of veneer, as some have such thin layers that they need a coat of French polish for protection.
C

This Victorian sideboard with carved decoration dates from about 1860. The carving is done by mechanical process and then applied. The plain mahogany veneer, which is thin and cut by mechanical means, is set on to a soft deal or pine carcass, and these versions need a close examination for worm. Drawers wear down easily, and sometimes replacement slides are needed.
C+

Victorian chiffoniers are usually quite small, with a staged section at the back of one or two shelves. Though by no means rare, they are beginning to become sought after by reason of their small size and shallowness. It is a classic example of Victorian parlour furniture. Always check for worm before buying.
E/F

Despite the high price of country furniture, a food hutch can still be found at fairly competitive prices. The majority of versions date from the early eighteenth century and are of crude country construction, made of oak, fruitwood or pine. These are often restored continually, but the presence of an old restoration should not materially diminish the value of the piece, and can sometimes enhance its interest. Oak and fruitwood examples are the more expensive, as are the scarce seventeenth-century versions.
H

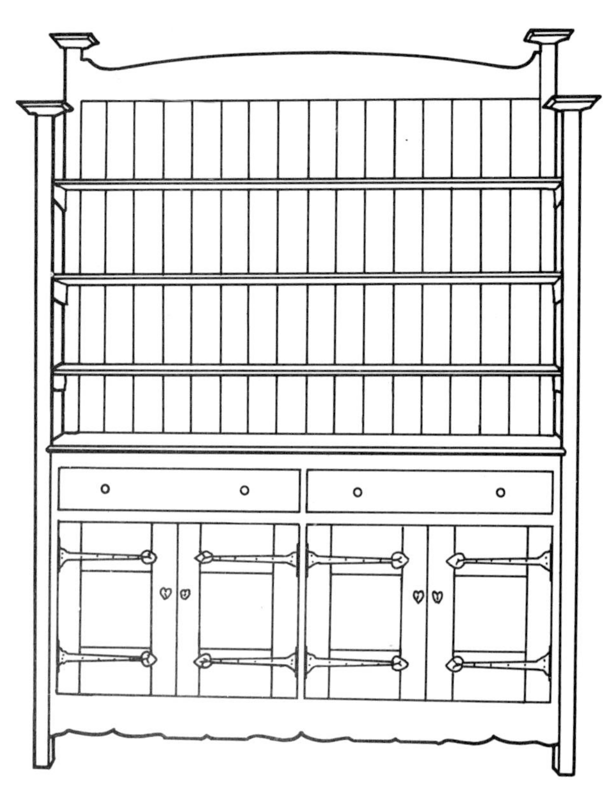

Expensive as dressers are it is still possible to buy nineteenth-century examples in pine for just under £750. The buyer is competing with an extensive and international market. This example is of good construction.
H

This type of bow fronted sideboard in mahogany dating from about 1820 survives in some numbers, though they are usually out of this price bracket. Only the more simple examples come within it, and they are recognisable by absence of stringing lines and rather stout appearance. A bow front, or a serpentine front, begins to put the piece over the £750 mark. But untypical examples, particularly if slightly later, with carving or especially with gadrooned work, represent better value.
H+

This is a good eighteenth-century oak dresser, with composite base and shelves. Period dressers in oak of fair quality start at about £1,100 and can cost several times that amount. They are good investments, are outstandingly practical and are one of the easiest pieces of furniture to resell. There is a large European and American market for English examples and dealers seldom keep them in stock for a long period.
K/L

This is a rare and fine quality mid-seventeenth-century court cupboard. These are much sought after and, as is the case with so much seventeenth-century oak, they are high in price, and this may well be taking into account some considerable restoration. The carving on many specimens has been added in the nineteenth century and although this affects the price, the European market is often prepared to take such pieces in preference to some plainer pure seventeenth-century examples.
L

The date of this fine mahogany sideboard is about 1790–1800. It is of the classic kind, with a cellaret drawer that is lead-lined and unconverted. The drawers and cupboards to these pieces have often been altered and the buyer should vigilantly enquire of the vendor what the state of the piece is.
K

Cabinets and Cupboards

THIS miscellaneous group of furniture concerns itself mainly with storage and display in the principal rooms of the house – the dining room and the sitting room. Although classic cabinets and cupboards are expensive the buyer of limited means can, with the exercise of a little ingenuity, manage to supply himself with interesting examples for a small outlay. In effect we are looking at an exceptionally wide area, especially in the lower price range. Remember that what looks small and undistinguished in the chaos of a junk shop can in a private house look remarkably successful.

Under £150	**£150–750**	**Over £750**
Pine corner cupboard	Edwardian cabinet	Italian vitrine
Pine kitchen cupboard	Corner cabinet	Gothic bookcase
Shop fitting	19th-century breakfront bookcase	Walnut bookcase
Bedroom cupboard	Mahogany wardrobe	Hepplewhite bureau bookcase
Victorian vitrine		

A simple pine corner cupboard makes best possible use of a very small space. This example dates from the late nineteenth century.
A

A standard pine cupboard with shelves, dating from about 1880, would originally have been painted. When stripped it would be useful in a kitchen.
B

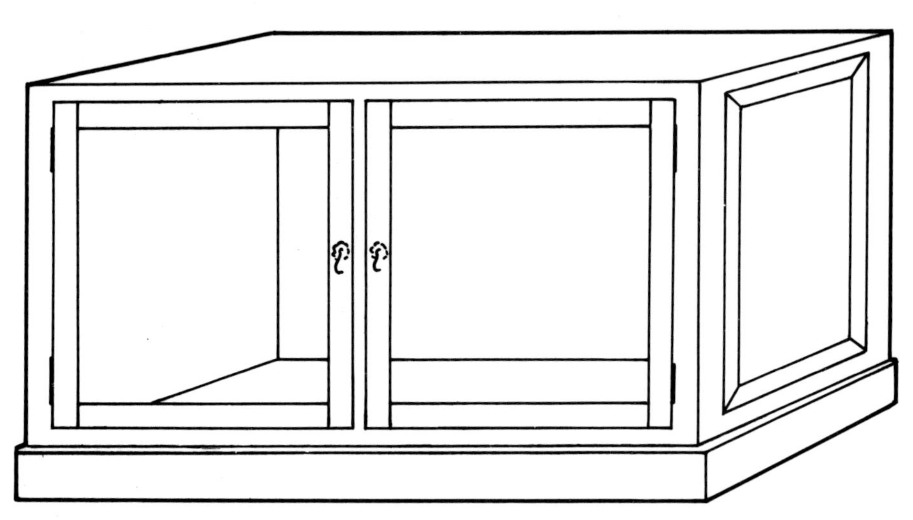

Although nowadays fairly uncommon, shop fittings are occasionally encountered in antique shops. In general a set of drawers from a chemist's shop is likely to be expensive, but this Edwardian glazed cupboard has some value.
B/C

This is a larger than usual version of a bedroom cupboard, clearly from an Edwardian suite of bedroom furniture. Although not outstandingly well made (the mahogany is veneered onto a pine or deal carcass too flimsy for the size) it represents an excellent buy. The usual inlaid marquetry neo-classical motifs are in this instance painted.
B/C

This late Victorian vitrine is ebonised, with gilt metal mounts and is of fair quality. They are quite often found in antique shops, used for display and seldom offered for sale. On balance they are fairly inexpensive and if they look somewhat dull in a shop, in a domestic setting they are seen to more advantage.
C

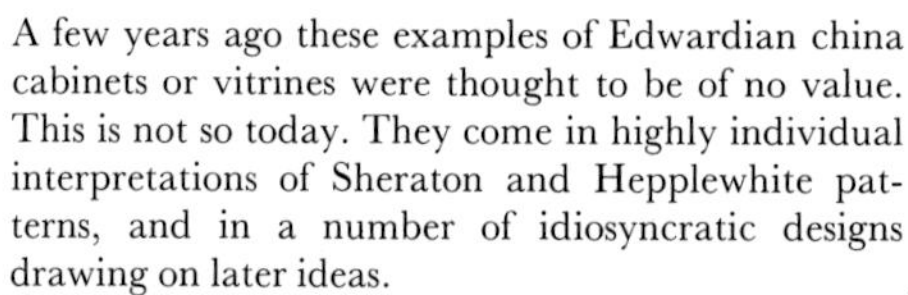

A few years ago these examples of Edwardian china cabinets or vitrines were thought to be of no value. This is not so today. They come in highly individual interpretations of Sheraton and Hepplewhite patterns, and in a number of idiosyncratic designs drawing on later ideas.
F

A simple glazed corner cabinet in two stages is one of the most desirable examples of antique furniture as it combines practicality with exceptional economy of space. The best examples can be very expensive. They were not greatly regarded by makers and designers, notably Chippendale. Check to see if the glazing bars are original. Less good examples, especially in fruitwood, come within the price range.
H

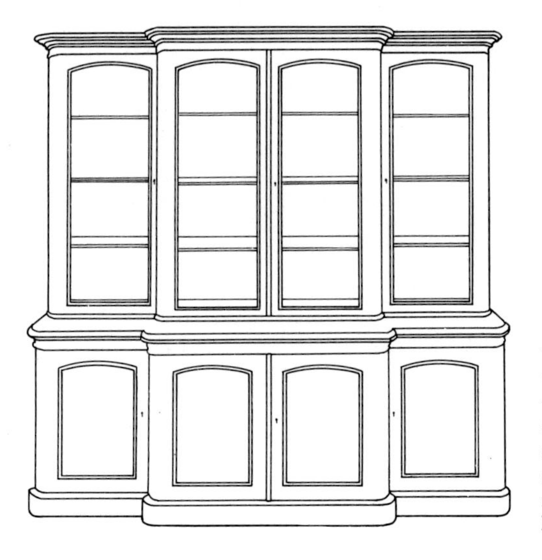

This simple mid-nineteenth-century bookcase has two stages and a breakfront. It is said that the light yellow-toned oak of which it is made was imported from Spain, but more likely from any number of sources. The lower section sometimes has cupboard doors as in this illustrated example, and sometimes not. By reason of their size they are not too expensive.
F

A mahogany wardrobe, with a chest of drawers below and hanging space above, constitutes excellent cupboard space in a large room. The generous proportions, notably the depth of some of these versions, make them less suitable in smaller spaces. Examples which retain their sliding shelves are best for general use as cupboards.
G

Right: This Venetian bombé vitrine dates from the late eighteenth century. Beware of modern copies—the lacquer work especially. This type of furniture is still made in Italy today.
K

Below: Large mid-eighteenth-century mahogany breakfront bookcases are also used today to display valuable collections, in particular china. This example has Gothic astragals or glazing bars. They are much sought after and therefore expensive. Some examples are 'made up', so beware.
L

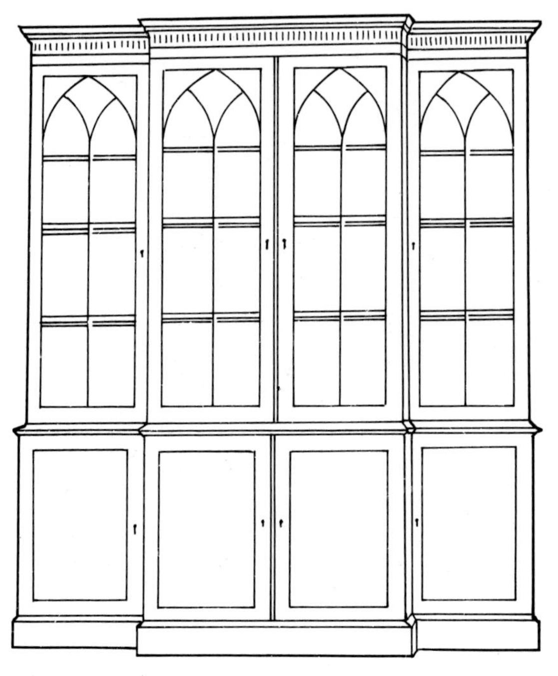

Right: A fine George I walnut cabinet is one of the most expensive pieces of furniture and is much collected. Condition makes a great deal of difference to the price.
M

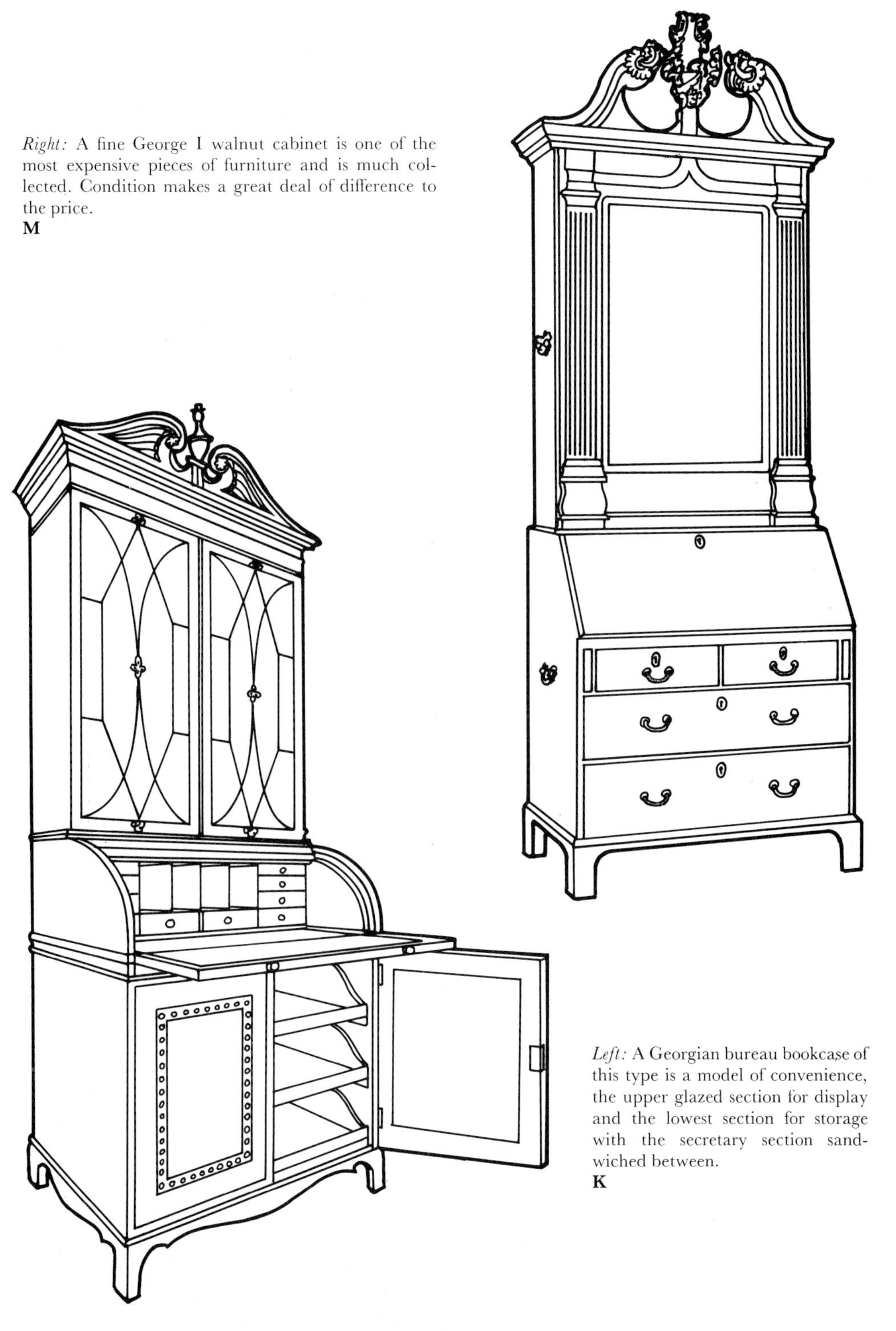

Left: A Georgian bureau bookcase of this type is a model of convenience, the upper glazed section for display and the lowest section for storage with the secretary section sandwiched between.
K

Wardrobes and Presses

IN the past few years wardrobes have been neglected in favour of 'fitted' cupboards. This preference usually means that the proportions of a room are destroyed by the fitting in of the cupboard, and although the cubic capacity is high, much of it is often useless because shelving and hanging space is not sensibly arranged. In addition, fitted cupboards are expensive.

These much despised wardrobes are, it is true, usually bulky, but are frequently well made (seldom to be said of the fitted cupboard). Hanging space is uncommon in early examples for clothes were folded and kept in chests and drawers, or hung in rooms designated for the purpose. The word wardrobe was not used to denote a hanging cupboard until the eighteenth century, before which the common expression was 'press'. Eighteenth-century examples have two stages, the lower a chest of drawers and the upper an enclosed cupboard, usually with slides and less commonly with pegs for hanging clothes. Many have been converted to take a hanging rail. Sheraton added wings with long hanging cupboards which allowed gowns to hang from recognisable clothes hangers. (Hangers were encountered regularly after 1850 but are rare before that date.)

Nineteenth-century wardrobes can be massive and elaborate. They usually break down into three or more pieces. Smaller examples often made for poorer households are very numerous and by no means expensive. Two factors affect the price: first, some pieces are made of exceptionally good quality wood and a restorer may buy them to cannibalise in order to restore another earlier piece of furniture; secondly, some three-stage wardrobes are now converted into breakfront cabinets and bookcases. In each case the price paid is higher than usual.

Wardrobes, and especially the Georgian presses, are now to be found in living rooms which can accommodate them, used as drinks cupboards and the like. They look extremely effective.

Under £150	**£150–750**	**Over £750**
Four Victorian wardrobes	Georgian pine press	Georgian oak hanging cupboard
	George III mahogany press	Norman armoire
	French armoire	Hepplewhite clothes press
	Circular wardrobe	
	Victorian three section wardrobe	
	Arts and Crafts wardrobe	

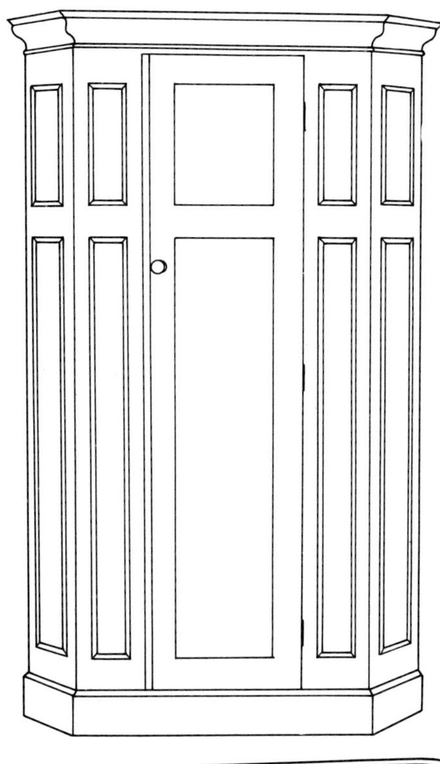

This is an elegant example of a stripped pine late nineteenth-century corner wardrobe. These not uncommon wardrobes often solve the problem of hanging space in an extremely small spare bedroom. Always watch for alterations, particularly with pine—cornices are very frequently replaced.
B

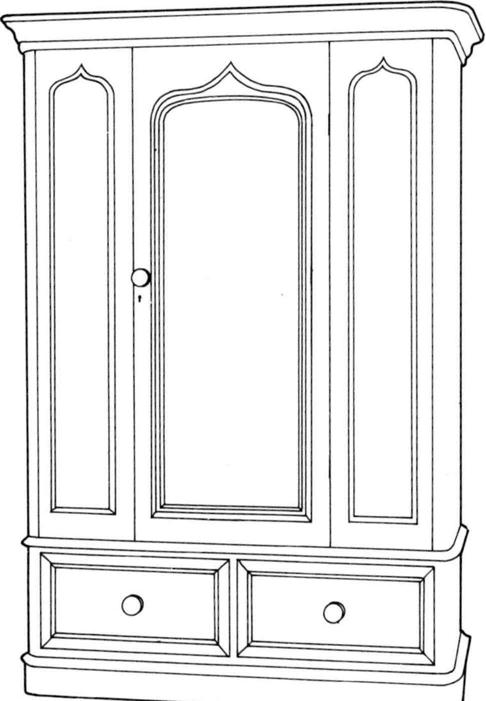

The original porcelain handles are a good feature of this type of pine wardrobe. The example illustrated has a mirrored door and drawers underneath and dates from about 1880.
B/C

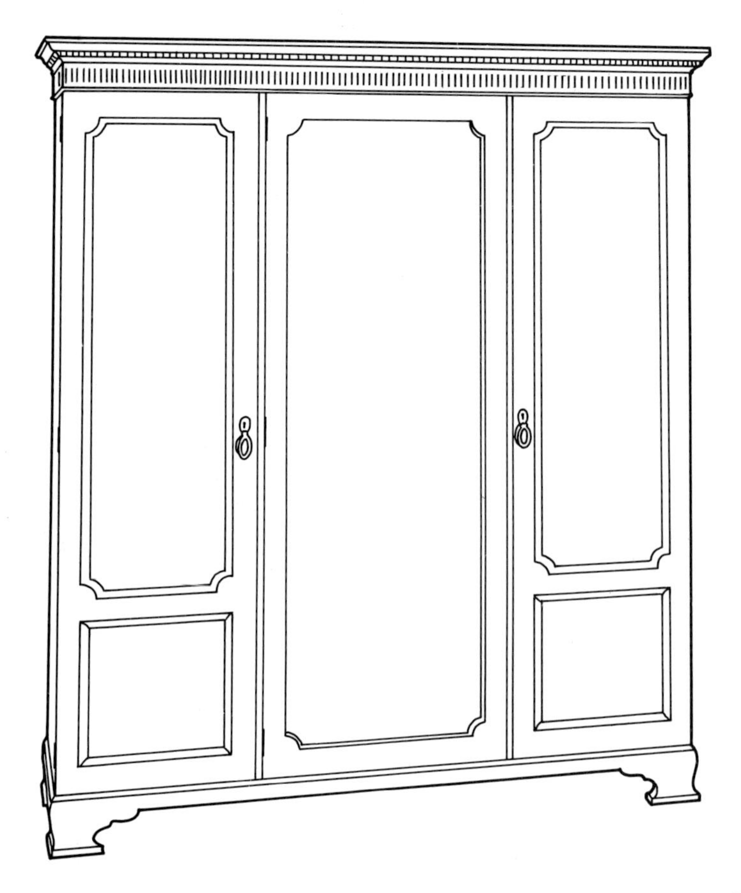

Above: A large mahogany three-section wardrobe dating from about 1880. A study of this piece, which incorporates in its design only eighteenth-century motifs, shows that it is possible to turn it into a breakfront bookcase for a small outlay. At auction a high price might be reached but under ordinary circumstances this style of furniture falls inside the lower price range.
C

Right: A design for a plain wardrobe of about 1882. Usually veneered in mahogany,. this example has some moulded work and the centre of the door panels is inlaid or painted with decoration. These are more commonly purchased at an auction or in a large antique furniture warehouse or repository.
B

Above: A linen press, originally with sliding trays in the top part, may sometimes have had this cupboard section converted into a hanging compartment. This example is of pine but it most likely started off life painted, possibly simulating a mahogany version. The thin ledge around the base of the hanging section is unusual. An example like this is likely to be used other than as a wardrobe.
F/G

Above right: This style of late Georgian mahogany wardrobe, with sliding trays in the upper section, was in use with only slight alterations from about 1760 to 1850. However it is usually possible to date them to within a few years by the smaller details of decoration found on them. A dealer may well be persuaded to put early handles on a piece and on this type of furniture they are often deceptive and convincing.
F–H

Right: A small French armoire (in effect a wardrobe), of provincial make and dating from the early nineteenth century, is popular as a hall cupboard or in dining or sitting rooms. Repairs are often found as the low cabriole feet tend to rot away and the back panelling to these cupboards is often very flimsy. They are found in oak, walnut or in the fruitwoods.
H

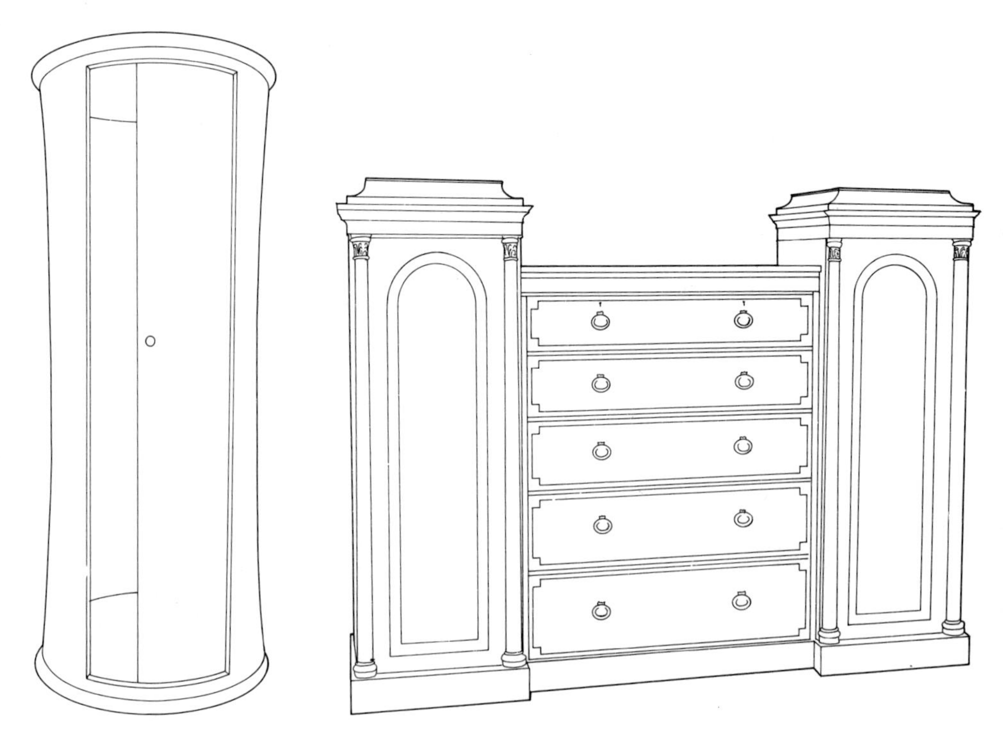

Above: A three stage wardrobe, the centre section a large chest of drawers supported on either side by hanging cupboards. This style of wardrobe is illustrated in Sheraton's *Cabinet-Maker and Upholsterer's Drawing Book 1794*, but the example illustrated dates from about 1880 and is veneered in good quality figured mahogany. By reason of its size this example is often sold for a fairly low sum.
G

Above left: An unusual circular wardrobe that is completely covered in chintz. Most of these wardrobes have a central hook and it seems likely that this would have been used to hang dresses. This example is probably mid-Victorian.
D/E

Left: An oak cupboard of about 1905 by Sir Ambrose Heal in the tradition of the Arts and Crafts movement. Lesser unattributed examples of this kind of furniture (often slightly later in date) are frequently to be had inexpensively in the repository type of shop.
C

It is often difficult to draw the distinction between a wardrobe or hall cubboard. This fine quality English example in oak dates from the early eighteenth century. The interior is fitted with hanging pegs and there is no sign of the shelving you would expect in a wardrobe ever having been present. Also, the use of a lower stage with cabriole legs is decidedly uncommon on a wardrobe. *Photo courtesy of John Keil.*
L

There is a surprising amount of French provincial furniture in the English market and it is currently being imported on a noteworthy scale. Good pieces are less usual and are found mostly in London and one or two sources in the country. Here is a good Norman armoire of the late eighteenth century in walnut. It has elegant carving and almost certainly would have been displayed in a public room, not a bedchamber.
L

This is a fine mahogany wardrobe of the period of George Hepplewhite. The essential shape of the ordinary wardrobe of the period is there, but the refinement of the carved applied decoration – which is rare – lifts this piece of furniture into the top class.
L

Miscellaneous

WHEN a room has been furnished with what for sake of convenience we call 'necessaries', that is in a dining room a table, chair and sideboard, or in a drawing room sofas, armchairs, display cabinets and bookcases, the collector is faced with the task of 'filling in'. Here there are no hard and fast rules. The collector may be a keen chess player, or card sharper, and clearly it is pleasing to have an interesting piece of furniture to enhance such pursuits. The keen gardener may wish to display some tender plants or shrubs in a jardinière or on a pedestal. The collector of china, glass or silver may choose a cabinet to emphasise the choicest examples. The musically minded may well choose a fine instrument which may well serve a rôle as a dominant piece of furniture. A bequest from a deceased relation may persuade the recipient to invest in a fine bracket clock, or a longcase clock.

Under £150	**£150–750**	**Over £750**
Georgian corner wash stand	Corner cupboard	Games table
Butcher's block	Wine cooler	Cheveret
Plate rack	Oriental hardwood table	Bracket clock
Bamboo canterbury	Regency jardinière	
Pole screen	Tantalus/trolley	
Overmantle mirror		
Wirework jardinière		
Games table		

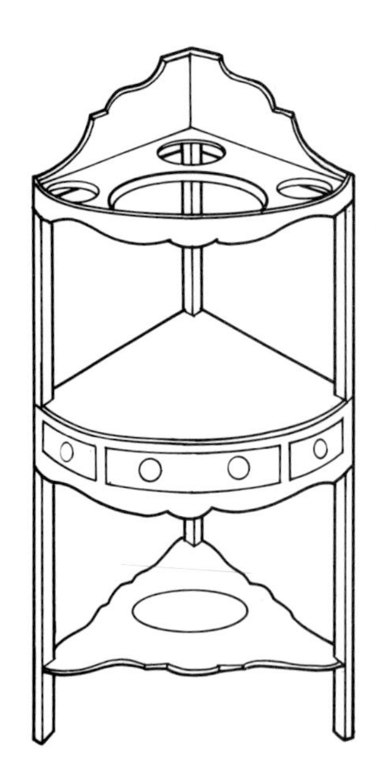

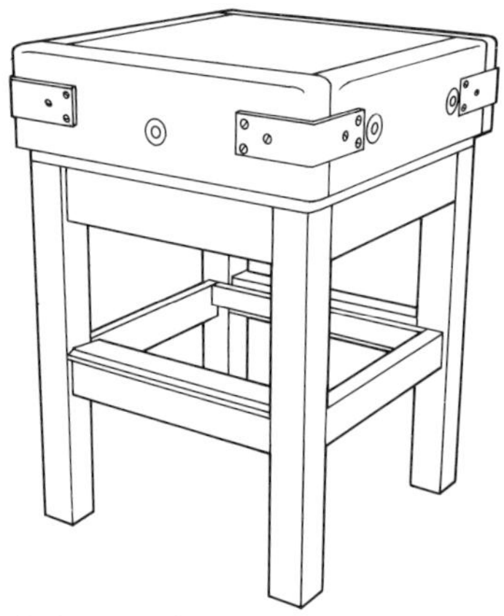

Left: This late nineteenth-century butcher's block may seem an extraordinary choice, but it can be extremely practical in a kitchen and would make a useful table in a cottage. Examples are usually inexpensive.
B

Left: A late Georgian corner wash stand in mahogany can be expensive in the hands of a first rate dealer, but they are known in the trade as being difficult to sell and can be found inexpensively in small antique shops and salerooms. The top has a high splash back and is usually pierced to hold a wash basin; sometimes dealers insert a mahogany quadrant to provide a plateau top.
C+

Below: Shelves intended for platters are quite common and are surprisingly inexpensive in comparison with the dresser bases over which they are often found. Seventeenth and eighteenth century oak examples would come into the middle price category, but pine and fruitwood versions of the eighteenth and nineteenth century are to be found less expensively, even in specialist shops.
C+

Right: Canterburies are very expensive as a rule, but the bamboo varieties are little collected and are obtainable for a much smaller sum of money. This example dates from about 1890 and as with almost all bamboo furniture of this period, provides good value for money.
A

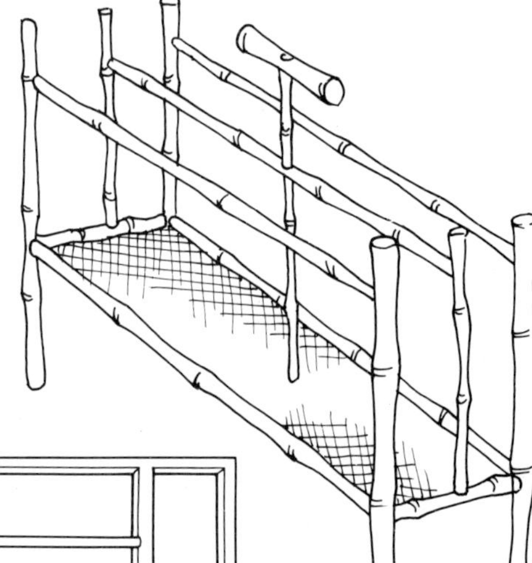

Above: Pole firescreens such as this Georgian example have often been converted into small tripod tables. The height of the screen is adjustable and it usually contains tapestry, which need not be expensive. Poles without screens can be found, often for slightly less money.
C

Top right: A small gilt overmantle mirror is a good buy in good condition; a late Georgian or William IV example as illustrated can still be had in the lowest price category. Damaged examples are even less expensive but are risky buys because of the problems of restoration.
C

Centre: Wirework jardinières exist in all shapes and sizes and in various stages of disrepair. Originally intended for the conservatory, today they are equally useful anywhere in the house. Elaborate versions can be very expensive, but the example illustrated, dating from about 1830, falls easily within the lowest category.
B

Right: Rectangular tables with inlaid chessboard patterns can be found veneered in mahogany, walnut or rosewood. The legs, although solid, are seldom in the same wood as the top but are stained to match. The example illustrated is light in weight, an indication that the carcass is probably deal rather than pine. It is veneered in walnut and has small floral groups in marquetry at either end.
C+

Above left: Although this mid-Georgian corner cupboard is simple, it is quite expensive because of the high quality of its construction. This example is in red walnut rather than mahogany. Glazed fronts, when genuine, make the cupboards even more expensive, as does a well fitted interior. Bow fronted examples (usually dating from about 1790 to 1800) should be carefully studied for damage as the curved fronts can be difficult to repair.
E–G

Above right: A typical hexagonal late eighteenth-century wine cooler. Examples continued to be made well into the nineteenth century. Often the lead lining has degenerated and the veneering worked loose but the example illustrated is in good unrestored condition. Sometimes wine coolers are converted into drinks cupboards and the like and any such alteration diminishes the value.
G

The low height of a nineteenth century Oriental hardwood table enables it to serve better than most European period tables for use as a coffee table. They are usually well made, using solid timber rather than veneering, and are richly carved. The joints are not typical of European furniture. Their best use, of course, is to display a collection of Orientalia.
H

Jardinières come in all shapes and sizes and it is always worth trying to find out if an example is original or if it has been converted from some other piece of furniture. This is a Regency version, in the form of a small table. The top slides away to reveal a tin lined or lead tray to contain the potted plants.
H+

This tantalus/trolley is in gilt metal and was made in the second half of the nineteenth century. It is unusual and for this reason is likely to be expensive. Antique trolleys are not usually available so are likely to be in considerable demand. The fact that it is particularly unusual will also make it expensive.
F–H

Above: This early nineteenth-century arched-top bracket clock is an excellent purchase, providing the mechanism is in good working order (English movements are very expensive to repair). This example has a verge escapement but most bracket clocks of this kind have anchor escapements. The case is mahogany with ebony bindings, especially well made, with good brass fish scale panels and an ornamental handle. In height it measures about 40 cm (16 in).
J+

Above left: This is a rare mid-nineteenth century example of a much collected piece of furniture, the games table. The top opens up to reveal a chess board on one side and a backgammon board on the other. Underneath are compartments for chessmen and draughts and backgammon pieces, gaming chips and cards. Even the less unusual and splendid examples will be found only in the top price category.
L

Left: A cheveret is a small ladies' writing table which is essentially portable. They were most commonly found in the last quarter of the eighteenth century and the example illustrated dates from about 1795. Usually they are made in satinwood or some other light coloured wood, and they are also light in weight. Typical collectors' pieces, their small size and elegant design make them very desirable for use in a small flat and therefore expensive.
K

PART THREE

A Short History of Furniture

THE third part of this book attempts to compress the major movements in furniture history into a small number of pages. It is a 'potted' guide. To deal with the subject in detail would require a great deal of space: each individual section could be expanded with ease into a full scale book of over 500 pages. But for the ordinary buyer of antiques this depth of knowledge is unnecessary and perhaps undesirable, possibly leading to the unhappy situation where it would be difficult to see the wood for the trees.

I have concentrated instead on the broad trends, and on isolating one or two typical features which the average buyer may find helpful. This results in some generalisation, but many antique dealers themselves rely on generalisation when they describe what they are selling; there is nothing wrong with it *per se*, providing it is informed. The section on oak, for instance, generalises when it speaks of an 'Age' in accordance with established practice, but it goes on to explain as clearly as possible that the use of oak was by no means confined to that period, as a visit to a modern furniture shop will prove. For a list of books covering the subject in more detail, consult the bibliography on page 158.

The time chart on page 156 gives a further guide to the overall relationship of respective periods of furniture. The Age of Mahogany should not be regarded as something unrelated to the Age of Walnut, or indeed Oak. It is equally important to realise that at any one time there was a relationship between the furniture that was being made in France and in Great Britain. Do not use the chart as a means of extracting 'dates', as if it were a school crib: much furniture cannot be dated with any precision and this is seldom important. The real value is that it denotes graphically the chronological relationship between the various movements, tying them up as neatly as possible. It makes immediately obvious, for instance, the fact that the Regency in England does not coincide with the Régence in France. Technical terms have been used only where necessary. Where they have been used, a definition has been given in the glossary on page 157.

THE AGE OF OAK

To say that there is a distinguishable Age of Oak is not to overlook the fact that oak is the British national wood and has at all times been in use for the manufacture of furniture. It was only in the years after World War II, when supplies became so depleted, that oak became a luxury wood.

England has probably imported oak from earliest times, for in the Middle Ages the transport of oak by sea from the Continent was probably cheaper than bringing it across land. Towards the end of the seventeenth century, supplies of good native oak became short, despite laws passed over a hundred years previously to conserve and increase stocks. Import became a significant factor, and such imported oak was known as 'wainscot', from the Dutch word *wagenschott* meaning 'wagon-borne'. At about the same time, the 1660s, England entered the Age of Walnut, but although the phrase the Age of Oak applies to the preponderance of furniture made before that date, oak furniture continued to be made in great quantities.

Oak remained popular, in particular, for less expensive London furniture and, most important of all, for country furniture (where changes in taste are slower and sometimes non-existent). It should also be realised that most walnut, mahogany and rosewood furniture, however grand, is veneered on to an oak or pine carcass, and this applied throughout the eighteenth and nineteenth centuries. By 1830 we encounter a mixture of revivalist styles (a trend known as historic revivalism, see page 146) and oak was again used on major pieces of fashionable furniture. Its use as a surface wood continues to the present day, although the timber available is almost certainly imported and is now so valuable that it is used very rarely except for veneering on a deal or chipboard carcass.

Construction and decoration

Early oak furniture exhibits the rudimentary methods of *joining*, mortise and tenon, pegged for strength. A mortise and tenon joint has a projecting section (tenon) which fits exactly into a cavity (mortise) on the piece of wood with which it is joined. The planks of wood were riven, not sawn, and smoothed by use of an adze. It is possible, despite the passage of time, to see how the wood was prepared, particularly in the less well finished backboards to items such as oak cupboards and dressers (remember these backboards may have been replaced, so beware). The earliest workers in oak who banded together as a union or guild were known as joiners, whose skill (or mystery, as they called it) was in the working of joints. The early Elizabethan stools, that represent the most available of sixteenth-century furniture for the general collector, are known as 'joynt' stools in reference to their construction.

The *carving* of oak furniture started in rudimentary ways and is seen in a small variety of forms of which the most usual is 'chip' carving, where small wedges of oak were chipped out of the surface of the piece of furniture (generally a chest) to form complex geometrical patterns. Elaborate gothic panels can be found, as can linenfold panels of varying quality. In the case of sixteenth-century oak, the survivors are often of ecclesiastical origin, but domestic specimens are also encountered. Oak, although a hardwood, is easily carved once the skill is acquired.

Turning was the third skill which materially affected the appearance of oak furniture. Its use was at a height from the middle of the sixteenth century and throughout the seventeenth. Turning also had its own guild to protect its interests. The skill is that of forming a limb of wood to a specific shape by chiselling it while it is being rotated at speed on a lathe. There are some chairs which are entirely constructed out of turned members. It is easier to produce a decorative effect by turning than by carving so as a rule turned examples are less grand, although there are well known exceptions.

Inlay on oak is not common: it is difficult to work with the greatest precision. But examples are found, floral in inspiration, on boxes and on panels in chair backs or cupboards. Except on fairly grand pieces, thin lines of inlay in ebony or boxwood are found only after about 1650.

Furniture design throughout the Age

Tudor furniture is rare and specimens using wood other than oak have not survived in any numbers at all. We know from inventories and specific reference in wills that furniture was valued and considered as fit for disposing of piece by piece. The furniture itself shows little development in the technical processes already known in mediaeval times, with the exception of the increased use of turning. For example, those large, bulbous-legged Elizabethan refectory tables had their legs turned on a lathe. The ideas of the Renaissance in Europe were slow to appear in England, but it is noticeable in some joint stools of the late sixteenth century that the legs are turned to resemble classical columns (albeit rather crudely). There is also a greater tendency to achieve harmony of proportions which was not especially evident in the fifteenth century. The roundel with a bust inserted is a carved feature which is classical in inspiration; this is called 'Romayne' work, but few specimens are genuine.

The later years of the reign of Elizabeth I are typified by a considerable exuberance of design which reflects the confidence of that period. The provincial examples of furniture begin to become much more showy and the bold designs of the wainscot chair from the north of England carry on well into the seventeenth century. But at the same time the London and court furniture of the reigns of James I and Charles I shows an increasing degree of severity, using plain undecorated columns on chairs or court cupboards.

So it is not true to say that the severer forms of domestic furniture of Cromwell's Commonwealth were entirely due to Puritanism, for a simplification had already started. It was during this period (1649–60) that there was some exploration of the variety of turning styles to decorate pieces of furniture. 'Bobbin' turning was initially the most usual and the term is largely self-descriptive. Perhaps a more inspired turner would introduce a thin fillet between the bobbins and we call the result 'reel and thread'. (Terminology does vary; a bobbin is sometimes called an 'egg'.) The final skill in turning was the 'twist' or 'barley sugar' leg which involves a fairly difficult technique and appears to have been introduced into this country from Holland. The most typical piece of furniture of the Commonwealth is the Cromwellian or farthingale chair, the characteristic form of which is a rectangular stuffed seat and upholstered back panel with four turned legs united at the base by four plain stretchers. Such chairs were upholstered with leather or tent stitch embroidery.

The Restoration of Charles II in 1660 marks the high point and also the cut-off point for the Age of Oak. Using Dutch models the furniture makers of this jubilant period made elaborate and elegant chairs and tables in oak using the techniques of carving, turning, caning (for caned seats had by then become common) and upholstery. Oak, however, survived as a fashionable wood for only a few more years, just into the reign of James II. With the reign of William and Mary came walnut, which is another age.

THE AGE OF WALNUT

There are Elizabethan records of the use of 'Walnuttree' but few survivors of that period; its appearance is uncommon before 1660 on English furniture. But by 1660 the supplies of English oak were getting very scarce and it may well be that walnut was used independently of any fashion because of this scarcity. Certainly walnut stocks were available, if not in great quantities. The demand for oak did not materially diminish, however, for it was needed as a carcass wood at a time when the demand for furniture was much greater than ever before. A sizeable quantity was imported. So the extent of the demand for walnut could be overstated: on a good veneered chest of drawers, for example, the proportion of oak is much higher than that of walnut.

Walnut is essentially a veneering wood and it is fairly unusual to find it in the solid, although a bachelor's chest is one example that often is, as are table tops. The two other occasions when walnut is necessarily used in the solid are when veneering is impractical (such as in the manufacture of chair legs, table legs and stretchers) and for such parts of a piece of furniture as need to be carved.

To produce a veneer was a skilled task. They were cut by hand with a specially shaped saw to a consistent thickness of 1.5–3 mm ($\frac{1}{16}$–$\frac{1}{8}$ in.). Once that skill had been mastered the workman had to be able to look at the block of wood from which the veneer was to be cut and decide how to make optimum use of the formation of the grain to produce several thicknesses of well-figured veneer.

Furniture design throughout the Age

Charles II walnut furniture copied what was fashionable in oak but surpassed it in popularity because of the more luxurious finish that was obtainable. More sophisticated conceptions in walnut of the popular type of oak caned back chair were the result of the published designs of the Huguenot Daniel Marot (1663–1752), but they are scarce and of the William and Mary period. Throughout this period Dutch cabinet makers perfected the crude marquetry that the English, earlier in the century, had practised on oak. They taught the English to inlay fine marquetry designs on walnut veneers – on the tops of tables, on drawers and on the limbs of chairs – in fact on the surface of any plain piece of furniture that merited it. The brilliant, often virtuoso, work of the cabinet makers of the period reached a high point in the work of Gerreit Jensen (c. 1680–1715), one of the Dutchmen who worked for Queen Mary, consort of William of Orange. (Note that by now 'cabinet maker' was the term for the most fashionable furniture makers – a term still current.) Jensen was capable of making complex arabesques of fine marquetry. Inlaid into walnut we can find boxwood, bone, ivory, mother of pearl, ebony, holly, sycamore or fruitwoods, some of which were stained to widen the range of colour effects. The ideas were largely taken from the Dutch but the styles were soon assimilated and made characteristically English; it is not difficult to distinguish one type of marquetry from the other. But unlike the Dutch who continued to use marquetry throughout the eighteenth century, the English largely avoided the use of the technique by the end of the first decade.

The brief period from about 1695 to 1710 is of the greatest importance in the development of English furniture. During this period an English national style was being evoked. Today, the wing armchair, the dining chair and the bureau all hark back directly to those few years. The taste for plain wood distinguished by its grain alone emerged first at this time. Queen Anne furniture also became a dominant style in the American colonies in the mid-eighteenth century.

The reign of Queen Anne (1704–1714) is the reign of walnut. Simple, uncomplicated forms are used, drawing later in the reign on the architectural principles we call Palladianism, a severe adaptation of purer classical styles. The outward appearance may seem simple but a wealth of understanding is involved in the mastery of the proportions that characterise this style of furniture. The cornice, a combination of mouldings that passes round the top of a cabinet is a complicated solution, but easily copied. The cabriole leg is an elegant form which came to its most perfect shape in the reign of Queen Anne.

By the time Queen Anne died there were a great many cabinet makers, set up in large establishments, who advertised their work and who occasionally labelled it. In London there was a large congregation near St Paul's Churchyard as well as in other locations. The overall quality of London pieces in a competitive world was high and we even have records of English furniture being exported to foreign countries such as Spain. The high standards and the competition between makers was to influence furniture for the rest of the century.

Walnut was beginning to be superseded: small imports of a new, dark red wood, mahogany, were beginning to be made up into furniture. Yet walnut had a final fling during the 1720s and 30s. Monumental Palladian furniture of the greatest purity became fashionable, employing strictly architectural motifs, highlighted with the use of carved giltwood (such furniture is often described as 'parcel-gilt'). The walnut used had a rich tone and a favoured variety known as red walnut is not uncommon. Dark burr veneers are also found. There is a school of thought which holds that this type of furniture is in fact the high point of all English furniture.

Mahogany was in general use by the end of the fourth decade of the eighteenth century. It was easily worked and had a consistent and restrained grain that was in keeping with the needs of the age. Walnut, the supplies of which must have been fairly well exhausted, was not in common use thereafter until the 1840s: it never again achieved the distinction of its heyday.

THE AGE OF MAHOGANY

When, in the years after 1720, mahogany arrived in the holds of ships coming from the West Indies, few could have imagined the importance it was to have in the history of English furniture. It was initially known as Jamaica wood, but there were other sources including Cuba, the Honduras and locations in Central and South America and the West Indies. In the second quarter of the nineteenth century supplies of African mahogany became available and certainly mahogany was known in and exported from the East Indies.

It was used because of its outstandingly even colour, which was a dark rich brown, slightly darker than red walnut which was enjoying a considerable vogue in the 1730s. It is sometimes difficult to distinguish between the two at a glance. Some varieties of mahogany have a marked grain and when the veneers are carefully matched make striking furniture. Walnut can seldom compete with the size and regularity of well matched mahogany veneers.

Furniture design throughout the Age

During the first period of mahogany furniture the wood was used in much the same way as walnut but it soon became clear that it was less inclined to split and when carved could show a degree of definition that was seldom achieved with walnut. The work of William Vile for instance (d. 1767), is outstanding because of a jewel-like brilliance to the carving of his furniture. But a maker of elaborately carved furniture might also produce simple case furniture of good quality – objects such as chests of drawers, bureau bookcases and presses.

In the 1750s there was a taste for rococo forms – elaborate curvaceous conceptions. Mahogany alone could be fashioned into these shapes without risk of damage. Numerous designs were made in this mid-eighteenth-century taste, and the most distinguished of all came from the pen of Thomas Chippendale (1718–1779) who in 1754 published *The Gentleman and Cabinet-Maker's Director*, which went into subsequent editions. The influence of Chippendale's designs was very great indeed, largely because they combined fancy with practicability, and watered down versions of his work appear even in country furniture. Chippendale's workshops in St Martin's Lane, London, manufactured fine quality furniture for many of the great houses in the capital and the provinces and a great deal survives.

Chippendale, however, had to adapt to the fact that his designs of the 1750s were in the course of time supplanted by the severer neo-classical designs of Robert Adam (1728–1792). In a businesslike way he soon altered the style of his furniture to take into account this new taste. The Age of Adam meant that mahogany, although used, was not always the first choice, for Adam favoured giltwood furniture (the wood gilded was invariably beech) and painted wood. Satinwood was also extremely popular towards the end of the century. This neo-classical furniture is typified by elegant swags and ribbons and the like. The chair back in the form of a shield is a motif we especially associate with Hepplewhite, another designer of the period (see page 56).

Thomas Sheraton (1751–1806) lends his name to the last era of the eighteenth century to employ mahogany on a large scale. He was a truly original designer and designed first light and feminine furniture then, towards the end of his life, furniture which is more Regency in flavour than eighteenth-century. Satinwood and rosewood are commonly found in addition to mahogany on the better pieces of furniture.

So throughout the last three-quarters of the eighteenth century good furniture was made in mahogany, and this accommodating wood lent itself to Palladian, rococo, neo-classical and early Regency furniture without difficulty. It was to continue as a major wood throughout the nineteenth century, holding its own against all comers, although the quality degenerated as supplies were depleted. As has been said, the import of African mahogany in the early years of Queen Victoria's reign helped to maintain supplies. So it is fair to say that the whole of the nineteenth century is also, in a sense, the age of mahogany, but the history of furniture is best served by breaking it down into other categories.

So wide and so varied have been the uses to which mahogany has been put that one can only treat the subject in the lightest outline, but remembering the sequence of rococo, neo-classic, and early Regency, and one or two basic forms, equips the collector with the basic material for identification.

THE REGENCY

George III had periodic bouts of madness and after 1809 was declared incapable of rule and his son George, Prince of Wales, became Prince Regent until his father's death in 1820. Technically this is the true 'Regency' period. But we use the expression to denote the furniture made in a period from 1800 to about 1830, the latter date conveniently being the occasion of the death of George IV. As a matter of interest, until a few years ago this was the date after which no manufactured furniture or other artefact could be deemed antique.

It is a significant period; the Regent's personal taste did much to give it a distinctive flavour. With the exception of Charles I he was the only member of the British monarchy to sponsor the arts diligently. But it would be wrong to assume that Regency furniture was wholly an expression of the Regent's taste: we know that he disliked many of the extreme examples and at the height of pure Regency he was buying French furniture some twenty years out of date.

In essence the Regency taste moved towards a purer and more simple conception of furniture. The same attitude was to be found in the France of the Directory (1795–1809) and the Empire. Roman was thought less pure than Greek, so a Greek emphasis is very much to be detected. Thorough scholarship produced some examples of remarkable congruence with the classical prototypes. Most scholarly, and highly influential, were the designs of Thomas Hope (1770–1831) published as *Household Furniture and Interior Decoration* in 1807. The line engravings which illustrate this work admirably depict the neo-Greek style.

The early years of the century were a time of military activity in the area of Egypt where Napoleon and Nelson were engaged in combat. This had the effect of exciting a wide interest in things Egyptian. This was taken up by designers like Thomas Hope, because Egyptian architecture (as Greek) had about it the elements of a primitive and pure style. This is why we find crocodiles and Egyptian masks on some pieces of Regency furniture. The interest was short lived, but a new purity was evident in furniture and persisted for a considerable number of years, certainly until the accession of Queen Victoria. Happily the crocodiles did not survive for so long.

These two tastes, for the Greek and for the Egyptian, are the main styles in Regency furniture. The sabre leg to a chair, often complemented with an arc back, is typically Greek. The use of cast and gilt metal mounts, and composition mounts, are also common. The wood most associated with the Regency is rosewood, with its striking dark and light striations. Mahogany was also extensively used. The taste was also for ebony stringing lines in Greek key patterns, quite thick and well defined. In essence there are few 'frills'. Also there were chairs and tables and other pieces of furniture painted to simulate rosewood, which was expensive and often not readily available. As usual the base wood for this painted furniture was beech. The extra lightness of beech made the chairs very portable.

In addition to the mainstream styles, there was a marked palate for Chinese artefacts. It is tempting to attribute all this to the spectacular pleasure dome of the Prince Regent, Brighton Pavilion. Much of it was clearly influenced by such a fantasy, but from the time of Charles II there have been attempts at creating furniture in the manner of the Chinese. The technique of japanning was devised to imitate the lacquer furniture of the Far East and much black japanned work is found from this period. Chippendale's designs show Chinese-inspired creations and Horace Walpole used the word 'sharawaggi' to denote these oriental fancies. But notwithstanding, Brighton Pavilion is a memorial to things Chinese, and also Indian (or Hindoo, as the expression was at the time). The domes of the Pavilion were in the Indian taste whereas the Music Room inside is the perfect expression of Regency Chinoiserie. Bamboo furniture was imported and also manufactured here in England and sometimes it is difficult to tell which is English and which is genuinely oriental.

The pure ideas of the early years were much watered down as they gained wider acceptance. The finer examples were more available because of some technical improvements in the manufacture of furniture. Machine-cut joints speeded up work without any great deterioration of quality, And the designs of Thomas Hope which catered for a rich and aristocratic public were copied by other men; a new and popular market opened up. George Smith, who was known as a flourishing cabinet maker from 1804, produced two important design books in 1812 and in 1826. They were clearly influenced by Hope but show designs which chronicle the decline of the purer ideas. Indeed it has to be admitted that some designs are overblown and ponderous.

With the death of George IV in 1830 his brother William IV ascended the throne. The general process of decline in Regency design continued, but some unusual pieces of furniture can be found which are derived from the bourgeois *Biedermeier* style in Austria and Germany. The sabre leg persisted, a model in clean lines; carving, although not fine, was seldom distorted as it was to become later in the century. So the period of William IV should not be lightly disregarded. There is much that is pleasing and valuable.

VICTORIAN FURNITURE

We now know that Victorian furniture is not all bad (as we were lead to believe a few years ago), nor mostly bad, but rather that thoughtlessly designed pieces are worthy of criticism. In fact the Victorians thought a great deal about design and in 1851 the Great Exhibition held in Hyde Park was a celebration of British invention and design and formed the prototype for exhibitions in other countries. What we must not look for is any consistency. There are no 'Ages' in the sense that there was an Age of Oak or Walnut. Various phases overlapped with, and existed independently of, each other. Sometimes influential designers, or even critics, expressed ideas that were taken up by a number of those independent movements, but it is, notwithstanding, proper to treat them all separately. There are five main areas: historic revivalism, the French taste, Japanese taste, Arts and Crafts, and Art Nouveau.

Historic revivalism

There are numerous explanations why the English should want to revive the past in the Victorian era. The most likely is that a middle class which was becoming richer and richer wanted to possess those artefacts of periods in which Britain had become great and was reassured by the sense of continuity. But there was also a great demand for comfort, because by the 1830s interior sprung upholstery had provided a degree of luxury previously hard to achieve.

GOTHIC FURNITURE The Gothic architectural period lasted from the twelfth to the sixteenth century and is typified by the pointed-arch style of buildings such as churches prevalent throughout western Europe. Only a few pieces of contemporary furniture have survived, the most notable being the Coronation chair in Westminster Abbey.

The first conscious imitation of the Gothic style was in the eighteenth century.

Strawberry Hill, designed by Horace Walpole in 1760, is a classic example. The lack of available research on the subject, however, resulted in artefacts which were certainly ornate but romantic in nature rather than authentic; these so-called Gothic motifs continued to be attached to chairs and bookcases until the end of the Regency period.

The Victorian revival was a more scholarly attempt at showing what Gothic furniture had really been like. Examples of the Gothic revival include St Pancras station, designed by Gilbert Scott, and the rebuilding of both the interior and exterior of the Houses of Parliament by A. W. N. Pugin (1812–52). Pugin's work there and the styles he promoted are more clearly defined and pure. Because the carving of many mass-produced pieces of Gothic revival furniture was not of good quality, people tended to forget how good the design was. Gothic ideas also played a part in the religious squabbles of High and Low Churches in the nineteenth century, and the ordinary churchgoer would have seen great changes in the second half of the century. Even Arts and Crafts furniture has some Gothic revival elements.

ELIZABETHAN FURNITURE Much historical study and manufacture of English furniture in the nineteenth century was in fact outstandingly unhistorical. A genuine Elizabethan chair, if it was called anything other than 'quaint', had about as much chance of being referred to as Gothic or Carolean. Some furniture made in oak was called Elizabethan but was generally nothing of the sort. Also, old oak furniture was selected for its plainness and recarved to give a rich, more 'antique' feel to it. Much old oak has been so badly recarved that it is probably more valid to call it Victorian than, say, Elizabethan. Students of catalogues of Victorian furniture will see chairs advertised that are loosely based on Charles II caned chairs in oak but declared in the catalogue to be Elizabethan, with upholstery.

PERIOD REPRODUCTIONS Some furniture copied the classic styles of the eighteenth century. This practice is of fairly long standing and there is evidence of it earlier in the nineteenth century than has been thought. Some London firms specialised in good reproductions, often made in near-identical ways to original specimens. But usually there is some giveaway – a proportion slightly awry or a small refinement which should not be there. Some reproductions do not pretend to be exact but are loose interpretations; a very short study of the real thing will show up inconsistencies. The signs of age will usually be present on a Victorian reproduction and this can make it very convincing. It certainly seems fair to say that more Chippendale chairs were made after 1800 and before 1914 than were ever made in the eighteenth century.

The French taste

English furniture has always been considerably influenced by that made in France and has copied or assimilated its characteristics. The nineteenth century treatment of French ideas in England reflects how France, and in particular Paris, was regarded as being a formative influence in taste. French styles were imitated as part of the historical revivalist process already outlined, but the latest styles were also copied. It is interesting to note that papier mâché furniture, which was very popular in the 1850s, drew very much on French styles for inspiration. The curvaceous forms of French furniture could be rendered with ease in this material.

Japanese taste

Japanese styles were parodied in the popular press but Anglo-Japanese exhibitions in the last quarter of the nineteenth century were outstandingly popular. It was a style traditionally favoured by the occupants of South Kensington and its influence was widespread. *The Mikado*, for instance, by Gilbert and Sullivan makes use of this vogue. In furniture it was advocated with great success by E. W. Godwin (1833–86) who built elegant and fine pieces of furniture (one is tempted to call them structures). His designs may be recognised by the interplay of ebonised wood with silvered fittings and leather panels. He also used fine painted white lines to pick out a design and sometimes achieved the same effect by gouging out thin lines and painting them in with dull gold. Such furniture is quite common, and frequently unrecognised.

Arts and Crafts

Much Victorian furniture was made by factory methods. Its indifferent quality in both design and manufacture was anathema to William Morris (1834–96). He thus had an affection for and advocated the revival of hand craftsmanship, which he felt had fallen on bad times. With colleagues such as Philip Webb, D. G. Rosetti and Ford Madox Brown (among others) he founded Morris and Company in 1862. This company designed and produced artefacts including furniture which re-emphasised hand craftsmanship. The 'Sussex' chair illustrated on page 53 is from his workshop, to his design, and possessed the integrity he felt had been lost. The designs draw on country crafts and mediaeval notions. Other makers followed on from this, notably Ernest Gimson (1864–1919) who, influenced by Morris, settled in the West of England and designed chairs on traditional principles – a ladderback by Gimson is the ultimate refinement in country furniture (see page 55). The tradition of craftsmanship is still thriving.

Art Nouveau

This was an international movement, revolutionary and not evolutionary, which sought to break away from traditional ideas by turning its back on regular form, preferring a curvilinear and sinuous structure. The style enjoyed a vogue from about 1885 to 1910 in England, and was particularly popular in Scotland. It did not lend itself too easily to large-scale manufacture of furniture, and when examples do appear the Art Nouveau form is normally superficial. The Scots, particularly of the Glasgow School, welcomed it and the movement had a noble advocate in the designs and manufactured furniture of Charles Rennie Mackintosh (1868–1928) whose reputation in Europe vastly exceeded English acclaim. The exaggerated forms which typify Art Nouveau are controlled in his case by a consistent regularity.

THE TWENTIETH CENTURY

You may wonder why a book which concerns itself in the main with antique furniture should mention the furniture of the twentieth century, furniture which is not antique by any subsisting definition. The answer is that it is collected. Some examples are commanding higher prices than most eighteenth-century furniture. A cabinet by Charles Rennie Mackintosh was recently sold for over £80,000, and Ruhlmann furniture can cost well into five figures. Since the term antique is now governed by age alone (assuming the 100 years rule for qualification) it is only a matter of some twenty years before twentieth-century furniture starts to become antique. The collector who hesitated would be a heavy loser and owners of modern pieces should think twice before they throw furniture out, or even sell it, for they may be selling to a percipient collector for a song.

Edwardian reproduction and later

Edwardian reproduction merely continued the high quality work that had been produced in the nineteenth century. Satinwood furniture copying Sheraton and Hepplewhite patterns with greater or lesser accuracy are quite common. The well known firm of Edwards and Roberts of London made excellent reproductions. Cheap labour and surviving technical skills meant that fine quality cabinet work could be carried out for quite low costs.

The years after World War II saw the interest in antique furniture quicken and be put on to a more scholarly basis. Large sums of money exchanged hands for good pieces of period furniture, in particular those made of early walnut and examples of high grade mid-eighteenth-century mahogany. Cheaper reproductions were made: machines copied in a cursory way the carving on oak dressers; George III sideboards were thinly veneered with cheap mahogany; elaborate decoration such as inlay was reduced to a minimum. Yet such pieces can fit in fairly inconspicuously with period furniture or, when used with other pieces of the same manufacture, create the illusion of a period interior. Reproduction furniture proliferated to the extent that today there are collectors who seek to create a complete reproduction interior in the belief that it is a genuine interior of, say, the twenties or thirties. Reproduction furniture is still made, some of outstandingly high quality, but the majority is indifferent. It is discussed in more detail in Chapter 3.

An individual designer

Although there are many designers of the twentieth century very few confine their interests to a purely nationalistic concept of furniture; they are nearly all international. I have chosen neither the most influential nor the most typical to represent them.

Eileen Gray was born in Ireland in 1879 and died in Paris in 1976. Before World War I she was making furniture and studied the art of lacquering in London and Paris. In 1912 her simple lacquered designs had been incorporated into a private scheme of interior decoration by Jacques Doucet, a Paris couturier. She is particularly remembered for her screens, usually lacquered, which first of all had the atmosphere of luxurious Art Deco about them (see below). Later her design became strikingly modernistic and economical, well in advance of Art Deco which by comparison appears almost meretricious. Her late pieces of furniture are masterpieces of engineering. Eileen Gray's work was little known even at the end of her long lifetime, and in the sixties designers were coming up with ideas she had produced in the mid-twenties.

There are others like her, many more influential. They do not fit easily into a concise abridgement of the history of furniture and because of their rarity their furniture is seldom seen except in museums and in the grandest private collections.

Art Deco

Art Deco is an amorphous taste in furniture belonging mainly to the late twenties and thirties. It draws on many sources but particularly on theatrical and balletic themes. At its grandest it was as expensive as any aristocratic furniture made in the past and the principal designers, who included Ruhlmann and Dunand, charged high prices. Below that level there was a commercial Art Deco which persisted throughout World War II. A good example of such a piece of furniture of the commercial kind is the late thirties wireless with the loudspeaker hidden behind a fretwork sunburst in veneered wood.

Twentieth-century traditionalism

Between reproduction and modernist furniture there was a style in England which drew extensively on the principles of the Arts and Crafts movement but which had adapted the ideas to modern commercial production. Sir Ambrose Heal and Sir Gordon Russell are the principal protagonists, and the Arts and Crafts movement had to acknowledge their elegantly simple, well made furniture.

Post war developments

In England the traditional Arts and Crafts movements exist side by side with modern designers in traditional materials. Both areas tend to be expensive so there is little wide commercial production. But ideas from Scandinavia, Italy and America are introducing new designs on commercial lines which employ both modern and traditional materials. In a few years we should be able to detect collecting areas.

COUNTRY FURNITURE

Standing often quite separately from mainstream antique furniture is that which has been made in the country by methods which have been much slower to change through the pressure of fashion or technical development. Historically this furniture has been sadly ignored, and the mobility of the population (who have taken furniture with them) and the lack of documentary evidence make it difficult to be wholly categorical or scholarly. But recently much research has taken place and we are beginning to get a picture of the origins, structure and range of country furniture.

With a small number of exceptions, country furniture and (for want of a better word) town furniture were constructed in much the same way until about 1660. The timber and methods of construction were the same. Mortise and tenon joints, turned limbs and carving were all technically similar. Regional characteristics had developed on a very localised scale and although our information is deficient we can speak of Salisbury and Yorkshire chairs, Lancashire chairs and Welsh dressers, as representing types which conform in a number of fairly conclusive ways. We have difficulty in dating country furniture with the same degree of accuracy as town pieces; fashions changed very much more slowly. Indeed with a piece of eighteenth-century country furniture it is rare that one is able to hazard a date within a quarter of a century, and even then one may still be wrong.

There is always a gradual assimilation of town features into country furniture. Country versions of bureaux, for example, in oak or a fruitwood, are soon found in the early years of the eighteenth century. A cabriole leg can be found on a country chair made in the reign of Queen Anne. But we must be careful not to date such furniture too early, for that same country chair is just as likely to have been made a good fifty years later.

Because country furniture's main purpose was to be functional rather than wholly stylish, we find numerous kinds of wood used in its manufacture. A maker might use an elm seat for a chair and beech or ash for the legs. Sometimes there was a good and traditional reason for such a choice; sometimes it was decided by what was available in the way of suitable timber. Examples are known of chairs which have six different woods indiscriminately used in their manufacture.

In the eighteenth century the technical advances of town furniture were adopted to some extent by country makers. Veneers, although not ordinarily encountered, do appear from time to time; one would normally expect a piece of country furniture to be in the solid. The point is that it is almost impossible to put forward any categorical rules.

By the nineteenth century even country furniture makers could be expected to have some mechanical aids. The example of the chair making industry centred around High Wycombe is of interest in this respect. Traditionally a woodman (called a bodger) lived in the beech woods around that town, cutting chair legs from the coppiced trees and turning them on a pole lathe. In the winter he made up the chairs himself or sold the pieces to the factories in Wycombe. Gradually as the nineteenth century progressed the bodger became redundant, and although many survived into the twentieth century, making the same type of leg, they had really been supplanted by machines. An experienced eye is required, however, to distinguish between some bodger-made chairs and those made by machine. A high regularity of detail was always required of the bodger, so this does not always solve the problem.

Country carpenters were a regular feature of every village throughout the nineteenth and into the twentieth centuries. Many survived World War II. Chairs, tables, cupboards or whatever made by such workmen are authentic country furniture and should be treated as such.

Finally, it should be noted that some country designs were taken up by major designers of furniture. William Morris, Philip Webb and others adopted these traditional patterns to such an extent that they were found in late nineteenth-century drawing rooms in London.

FOUR INFLUENTIAL INTERIORS

The history of interior design is not the same thing as the history of furniture. Neither is it an indication of the way in which every house was furnished. It does, however, provide us with some admirable examples of successful solutions to the problems of furnishing a room. I have taken four typical interiors, depicting major types of room setting existing between 1650 and 1900. They are illustrated and described in chronological order, as follows:

1 A country room furnished with a mixture of classic country furniture
2 A middle class parlour in a town house of the last years of the reign of Queen Anne
3 A good George III dining room of the early nineteenth century
4 A Victorian parlour of the last quarter of the nineteenth century

Chapter 5 of Part I deals in detail with ways of achieving a harmonious blend of antique and modern furniture. What is particularly interesting about these four rooms is that they are examples of period interiors that could be re-created today, without too much trouble and not necessarily at great expense. Rooms one and four could be put together by buyers who were restricted to the lower price band, as set out in Part II (with one or two exceptions). Room three contains medium as well as expensive furniture while room two comes exclusively into the top price bracket. Number one has a good deal in common with furniture from the Age of Oak (see page 139), number two is furnished with examples from the Age of Walnut (see page 141), number three fits in conveniently with the Age of Mahogany (see page 143) and number four is crammed with typical Victorian pieces (see page 146).

1. Country furniture

This interior should be visualised in a small farmhouse with whitewashed walls and exposed beams in keeping with the general appearance of a late seventeenth-century yeoman's dwelling. The main architectural feature is a large inglenook fireplace. This type of interior, although essentially of the late seventeenth century, persisted throughout the eighteenth and almost entirely through the nineteenth centuries. Although we expect to find mainly oak, elm, ash, fruitwoods and pine are also evident. The table is pine, late nineteenth century (see page 59); the dresser is in oak and eighteenth century (see page 117); the Windsor chair is early nineteenth century (see page 55); the joint stool is oak and mid-seventeenth century; the elm stickback chair dates from about 1800 and the smoker's bow from the mid-nineteenth century (see page 53). The simple pine dresser base is nineteenth century (see page 113).

All of these pieces, although not stylistically similar, are essentially country in flavour and as a result go together remarkably well. They are gathered together artificially in this drawing but it would not have been surprising to have found them all in the same room at the end of the last century. Similarly a yeoman farmer of the late seventeenth century

would not have found any of this furniture outlandish. Today it would make an informal room ideal for robust family living.

2. Queen Anne

The interior of this room is panelled, almost certainly with pine, but the pine has been painted over. The panelling is of good quality, with egg and dart carved moulding. There are plain oak floorboards, swept clean and unpolished. The essence of the room is its architectural quality, without grandeur or pretension.

The simple Queen Anne side chairs are in walnut, about 1710 (see page 56); the wing armchair is upholstered in a restored contemporary tent stitch, about 1714 (see page 69); the walnut cabinet is of a slightly later date, about 1720 (see page 125); the George I gateleg table, yet again in walnut, is of very fine quality (see page 63); the walnut bureau is an earlier version of the example illustrated on page 83.

Here you will see that there is a greater degree of consistency in the period details, and the wood used is entirely walnut veneer. But each piece of furniture would have been made by an individual craftsman working, we may assume, on his own initiative. Few people could afford to create a room of this quality today. We call this type of interior Palladian, but it is a humble version. It was the grand examples that ushered in the age of the designers, of whom the most famous was to be Robert Adam.

3. A Georgian mahogany dining room, about 1805

This room is of more expansive proportions than the Queen Anne parlour and is very lightly decorated with a dado rail with Greek key patterns. The doors are in figured mahogany.

The large dining room table is of a good size (see page 63); the mahogany chairs have sabre legs and are also about 1805 (see page 55); the sideboard is also in mahogany, but dates from the last years of the eighteenth century (see page 118); the hexagonal wine cooler is again in mahogany, about 1790–1810 (see page 136).

Although we would really expect these pieces to be in mahogany, we might just find one or two examples such as the chairs in rosewood, for the period is particularly noted for its fondness for dark highly figured woods of this kind. Again this would be an expensive room, but less so than number two as more of these pieces are widely available.

4. A late Victorian parlour

This small room has a cast iron hob to the conspicuous chimney piece and the simple proportions are somewhat confused by the general clutter. The effect is indeed largely achieved by the accumulation of inexpensive decorative china and glass and the sentimental prints on the wall.

The Grandfather chair dates from about 1870 (see page 67); the chesterfield sofa is sprung and well stuffed and was made for long periods (see page 72); the chiffonier in African mahogany dates from about 1860 but has overtones of some years before (see page 115); the balloon back chairs in mahogany are late 1840s (see page 54); the Sutherland table dates from about 1880 (see page 59).

Most of the things illustrated here are inexpensive and with luck can be picked up for a modest outlay. The variety of late Victorian furniture is remarkable, and these examples are mainly quite ordinary and available.

A Basic Time Chart

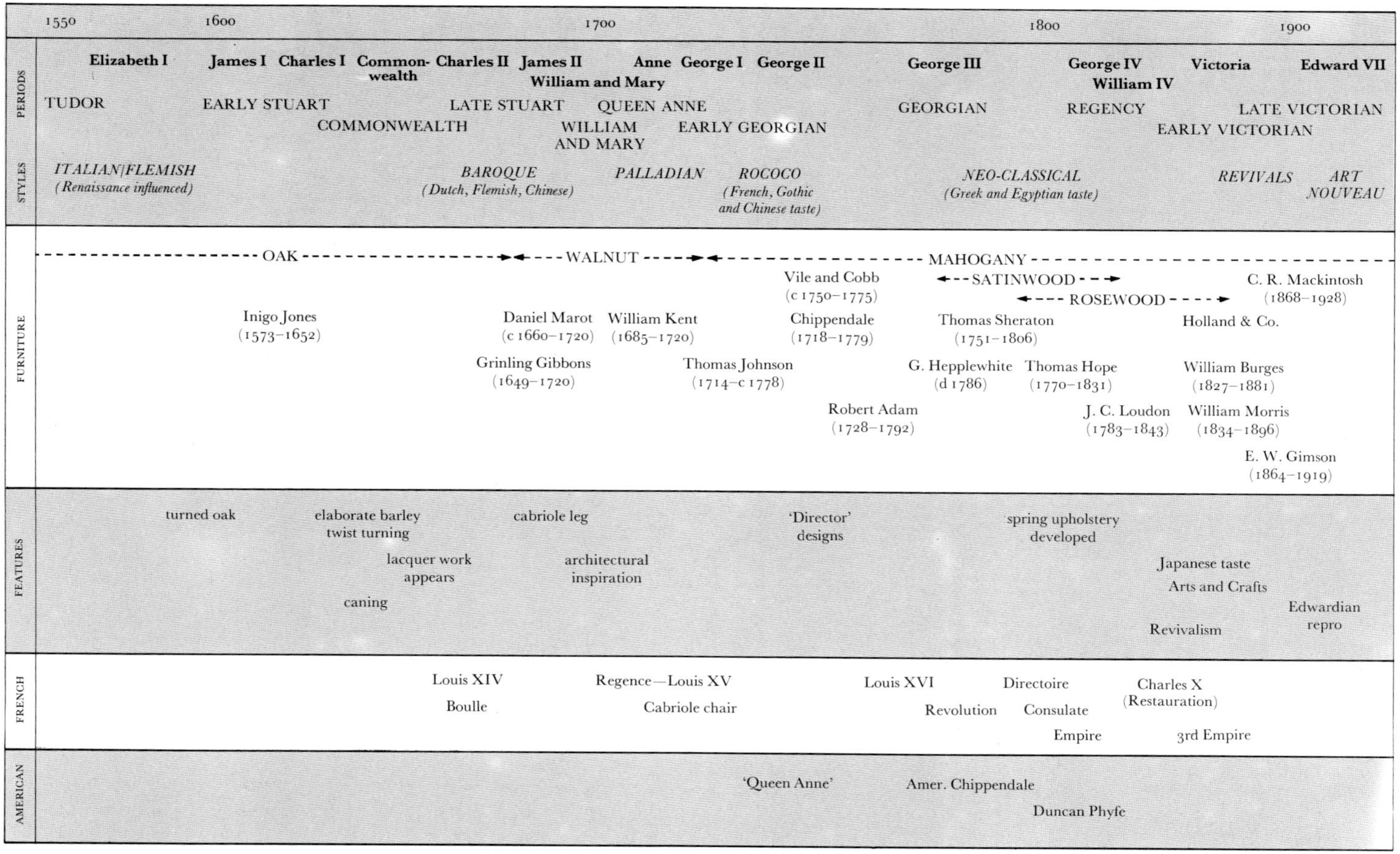

	1550	1600	1700	1800	1900

PERIODS

Elizabeth I · James I · Charles I · Commonwealth · Charles II · James II · William and Mary · Anne · George I · George II · George III · George IV · William IV · Victoria · Edward VII

TUDOR · EARLY STUART · COMMONWEALTH · LATE STUART · WILLIAM AND MARY · QUEEN ANNE · EARLY GEORGIAN · GEORGIAN · REGENCY · EARLY VICTORIAN · LATE VICTORIAN

STYLES

ITALIAN/FLEMISH *(Renaissance influenced)* · *BAROQUE* *(Dutch, Flemish, Chinese)* · *PALLADIAN* · *ROCOCO* *(French, Gothic and Chinese taste)* · *NEO-CLASSICAL* *(Greek and Egyptian taste)* · *REVIVALS* · *ART NOUVEAU*

FURNITURE

- - - - OAK - - - -→←- - - WALNUT - - -→←- - - MAHOGANY - - - -

←- - SATINWOOD - -→

←- - - ROSEWOOD - - - -→

Inigo Jones (1573–1652)
Grinling Gibbons (1649–1720)
Daniel Marot (c 1660–1720)
William Kent (1685–1720)
Thomas Johnson (1714–c 1778)
Vile and Cobb (c 1750–1775)
Chippendale (1718–1779)
Robert Adam (1728–1792)
Thomas Sheraton (1751–1806)
G. Hepplewhite (d 1786)
Thomas Hope (1770–1831)
J. C. Loudon (1783–1843)
C. R. Mackintosh (1868–1928)
Holland & Co.
William Burges (1827–1881)
William Morris (1834–1896)
E. W. Gimson (1864–1919)

FEATURES

turned oak
elaborate barley twist turning
lacquer work appears
caning
cabriole leg
architectural inspiration
'Director' designs
spring upholstery developed
Japanese taste
Arts and Crafts
Revivalism
Edwardian repro

FRENCH

Louis XIV
Boulle
Regence—Louis XV
Cabriole chair
Louis XVI
Revolution
Directoire
Consulate
Empire
Charles X (Restauration)
3rd Empire

AMERICAN

'Queen Anne'
Amer. Chippendale
Duncan Phyfe

Glossary of Some Terms Used in this Book

Balloon-back Form of chair back in shape of a balloon, early Victorian and later, hollow or upholstered.
Bamboo Hollow-stemmed wood (actually an oriental grass) popular from the second half of the 18th century in the making of European chinoiserie.
Barley-sugar twist turning Typical turning of the second half of 17th century, resembling barley sugar stick in shape. This type of turning was extensively revived in 19th century.
Beech Light coloured native wood, used mainly for giltwood furniture; also painted to simulate other woods.
Bentwood Strong cheap furniture using wood bent into shape by a steam process, developed in Austria in the 19th century but soon international.
Bombé Curvaceous form found on furniture, particularly European, originating from baroque notions.
Breakfast table Small rectangular or oval table, usually on pedestal and often tip-top, especially popular in late 18th-century and Regency England.
Buttoning Feature of upholstery, stabilising well stuffed work and usually very ornamental. Victorian deep buttoning was very pronounced.
Cabriole legs Elegant curving leg, bulbous at the top and tapering in an elegant curve to a foot often in the form of a pad or ball-and-claw. Square cabriole legs are the same shape, but in cross-section square.
Caning Method of upholstery using woven cane, for the seats and backs of chairs. Popular in France and late 17th-century England.
Canted A truncation to a corner or a square edge to a piece of furniture.
Chaise longue A sofa with an arm at one end only, usually well upholstered, originally French but much adopted by the Victorians.
Chamfered Similar to canted (q.v.); generally denotes some alteration to a plane.
Chesterfield sofa Originally a Victorian sofa, often button backed, with arms and back heavily upholstered and of the same height.
Commode Essentially a chest of drawers, originating in France in the late 17th century, but by the 19th century described, alternatively, a night cupboard.
Cross-banding A band of veneer often found around the edge of a table, the grain of which runs in an opposite direction to the grain of the surrounding veneer.
Ebonise This is a process of staining wood to resemble ebony, but the term is sometimes loosely extended to some types of black painting.
Escutcheons Originally an heraldic term, it also describes the key plates on furniture.
Figuring The pattern thrown up on the surface of wood by the cellular structure of the wood and by the growth patterns. It differs from wood to wood and with the method of cutting.
Fruitwood A generic expression for various kinds of fruiting trees, for example apple, pear, cherry, plum, peach, but not walnut or yew.
Gate-leg table A table with drop leaves supported by a gate contrivance which folds underneath when the flaps are not raised.
Gilt-metal Some metal mounts to furniture are gilded with pure gold (ormolu) but most are dipped in nitric acid and varnished, the effect being an adequate approximation. Expression used to distinguish a number of techniques from genuine ormolu.
Giltwood Carved wood is gilded in two ways, by the oil and by the water process; the latter is the more common and is brighter in finish.
Gothic Though originally a term of abuse (gothic = barbarous) it came to mean an elegant decorative interpretation of some gothic features. By the 19th century a more scholarly approach was employed by designers such as A. W. N. Pugin, who designed the interior of the Houses of Parliament.
Interior sprung 18th and early 19th century upholstery was basically a sequence of padding, but in the early 19th century springs were inserted, a technique forming the basis of upholstery to this day.
Ladder-back chair A type of chair back with horizontal splats in ladder formation. Usually associated with country chairs, but there are some fine 18th century specimens.
Lath-back chair A type of chair back with vertical lath splats usually found on the cheaper kind of 19th century Windsor chair.
Mahogany A hard red close-grained wood imported from the West Indies from about 1720 onwards and much favoured by cabinet makers. West Indian supplies were augmented in later years by imports from Africa and the East Indies. Excellent for carving and veneering.
Marquetry A skilled technique of inlaying woods with other woods of a different colour or grain to produce intricate designs. A feature especially of late 17th century English furniture and typical of Dutch work for a much wider period.
Oak Native wood of Northern Europe, silver grey when cut and seasoned but which with use takes on a dark brown, often nearly black, colour. Has distinctive flecks to the grain.
Pad foot A simple foot in the form of a pad popular in the first half of the 18th century.
Palladian A style of architecture with manifestations in furniture, deriving its name from the 16th century architect Andrea Palladio who employed classical Roman architectural concepts with great attention to proportion. Current in furniture from about 1720–50.
Parcel-gilt Gilding applied only to part of wooden furniture, often characteristic of Palladian furniture.
Patina A decorative 'skin' which covers the surface of furniture, the result of care and polishing.
Pembroke table A small drop-leaf table, rectangular in shape, the flaps usually supported by flaps in the undercarriage. Mainly late 18th/early 19th century.
Rails Generally, the horizontal members of furniture, particularly of chairs and tables.
Rope twist Turned work in the manner of rope, found on Regency furniture (although not exclusively so) and particularly on chair backs.
Rosewood A South American and East Indian hardwood, dark in colour with distinctive streaks. Most popular during the Regency.

Sabre legs Late 18th-century leg which continued well into the 19th century, with outswept sabre-like shape.
Saddle seat Solid wooden seat with a depression in the manner of a saddle.
Satinwood Fine golden yellow wood used in the neo-classical style of furniture of the later part of the 18th century. It was also popular with the Victorian designers. Not to be confused with sycamore, a light, lightweight and cheaper wood.
Shield-back A common style of chair back utilised by Hepplewhite and Sheraton in particular, representing a typical heraldic shield form.
Simulated woods Many woods were simulated, usually on a beechwood base, for economy or because they were too difficult to work.
Smoker's bow A variant of a Windsor chair.
Sofa Basically a chair seating more than one person, usually upholstered but not necessarily so.
Splats Wooden members joining the seat with the top rail of a chair.
Squab A loose cushion, usually shaped, to fit on to chairs, day beds, etc, and particularly employed when the furniture has a caned seat.
Stick-back Splats in the form of simple sticks, found on some Hepplewhite and commonly on Windsor chairs.
Stretchers Horizontal rails connecting and stabilising lower parts of the legs of chairs, tables and stands.
Stringing Thin lines of wood, usually box or ebony, are inlaid into furniture and when very thin this is known as stringing.
Sussex chair A chair produced by Morris and Company in the last quarter of the 19th century, based on a country prototype but essentially of the Arts and Crafts movement.
Sutherland table A variant of the Pembroke table (q.v.) but the flaps are extremely wide and when down, the table that remains is very narrow indeed, only a few inches wide.
Trafalgar chair A Regency chair with rope twist back and sabre legs, somewhat erroneously associated with the Battle in 1805.
Turning A technique of decorating furniture by rotating it at speed on an axis and carving it with a chisel.
Utility furniture Economy furniture made during and just after World War II, of simple but good design and robust construction.
Upholstery A system of padding furniture to increase its comfort.
Vitrine A glazed display cabinet, usually continental in origin.
Walnut A species of rich brown wood typical of southern European countries, but encountered in the North and in North America also. It has a rich golden colour and the figure is very marked. Burr veneers are prized. It carves well. Most popular in England from 1650–1730.
Windsor chair A wide range of chairs united by the feature that all the members (legs, arms, splats etc) joint into the seat of the chair.

A Selection of Books for Further Reading

AGIUS, P. *British Furniture 1880–1915*, Antique Collectors' Club 1978
ASLIN, E. *Nineteenth Century English Furniture*, Faber 1962
BILLICLIFFE, R. *Charles Rennie Mackintosh: Complete Furniture, Furniture Drawings and Interior Designs*, Lutterworth 1979
CHINNERY, V. *Oak Furniture*, Antique Collectors' Club 1980
CHIPPENDALE, T. *The Gentleman and Cabinetmaker's Director*, London 1754
COLERIDGE, A. *Chippendale Furniture*, Faber 1968
EDWARDS, R. (AND M. JOURDAIN) *Georgian Cabinet Makers*, 1955
Shorter Dictionary of English Furniture, Country Life 1964
FASTNEDGE, R. *Sheraton Furniture*, Faber 1962
FILBEE, M. *Dictionary of Country Furniture*, Connoisseur 1977
GILBERT, C. *The Life and Work of Thomas Chippendale*, Christies/Studio Vista 1978
Furniture at Temple Newsam and Lotherton Hall, National Art-Collections Fund/Leeds Art Collections 1979
GLOAG, J. *A Short Dictionary of Furniture*, Allen and Unwin 1969
HAYWARD, C. H. *English Period Furniture*, Evans 1977
Antique or Fake?, Evans 1970
HAYWARD, H. (Ed.) *World Furniture*, Hamlyn 1975
HEPPLEWHITE, G. *The Cabinet-Maker's and Upholsterer's Guide*, London 1794
H.M.S.O. *The English Chair*, 1976
INCE AND MAYHEW *The Universal System of Household Furniture*, London 1762
JENNINGS, C. *English Chests*, H.M.S.O.
JOY, E. T. *English Furniture 1800–1851*, Sotheby Parke Bennet/Ward Lock 1977
Furniture, Connoisseur, 1972
JOURDAIN, M. *Regency Furniture*, Country Life 1949
LEWIS HINCKLEY, F. *A Directory of Historic Cabinet Woods*, Bonanza Books, N.Y. 1960
MACQUOID, P. and R. EDWARDS *The Dictionary of English Furniture*, Country Life 1954
PEVSNER, N. *Pioneers of Modern Design*, Penguin 1960
SHEARER *The Cabinet-maker's Book of Prices*, London 1788
SHERATON, T. *Cabinet Dictionary*, London 1803
The Cabinet-Maker and Upholsterer's Drawing Book, London 1791
SPARKES, I. *The English Country Chair*, Spur Books 1973
STALKER AND PARKER *A Treatise on Japanning and Varnishing*, Oxford 1688
SYMONDS, R. W. *The Present State of English Furniture*, Duckworth 1921

Index

Illustrations are in **bold** type